D0903546

EDITING MODERN ECONOMISTS

Previous Conference Publications

EDITING MODERN ECONOMISTS

Papers given at the Twenty-Second Annual
Conference on Editorial Problems
University of Toronto
7–8 November 1986

EDITED BY

D.E. MOGGRIDGE

AMS PRESS, INC.
New York

Library of Congress Cataloging-in-Publication Data

Conference on Editorial Problems (22nd : 1986 : University
of Toronto)
Editing modern economists.

Bibliography: p.
Includes index.
1. Economics Literature—Editing—Congresses.
I. Moggridge, D. E. (Donald Edward), 1943-
II. Title.
HB199.C64   1988   808'.02   87-45817
ISBN 0-404-63672-1

Copyright © 1988 by AMS Press, Inc.

Published by
AMS Press, Inc.
56 East 13th Street
New York, N.Y. 10003

MANUFACTURED IN THE UNITED STATES OF AMERICA

Contents

Notes on Contributors

R.D. COLLISON BLACK, Professor Emeritus in the Department of Economics in the Queen's University of Belfast, author of numerous books and articles on the history of economic thought, was editor of the seven volume edition of *Papers and Correspondence of William Stanley Jevons* (1972–81).

SUSAN HOWSON, Associate Professor of Economics in the University of Toronto, author of several studies in twentieth century British monetary history and (with Donald Winch) *The Economic Advisory Council 1930–1939: A Study of Economic Advice During Depression and Recovery* (1977), is currently involved in editing *The Collected Papers of James Meade*, the first volume of which will appear in 1987, and in editions of the diaries of James Meade and Lionel Robbins.

CONTRIBUTORS

DONALD MOGGRIDGE, Professor of Economics in the University of Toronto, is joint Managing Editor of *The Collected Writings of John Maynard Keynes* (1971–), twenty-nine volumes of which have appeared, and is also involved in forthcoming editions of the diaries of James Meade and Lionel Robbins.

T.K. RYMES, Professor of Economics in Carleton University, author of several articles and a book in economic theory and applied economics, is currently involved in editing *Keynes's Lectures 1932–35: Notes of a Representative Student* which will appear in 1988.

JOHN K. WHITAKER, Professor of Economics in the University of Virginia, author of many articles in economic theory and its history, has edited *The Early Economic Writings of Alfred Marshall* (1975) and is currently at work on an edition of Marshall's correspondence which should appear in 1989.

Introduction

D.E. Moggridge

'Editing Modern Economists', the topic chosen for the twenty-second Conference on Editorial Problems, while reflecting recent trends, also represents a departure from past practice. The element of continuity comes in the decision not to consider a particular type of text – correspondence, novel, illustrated book – but rather an area of intellectual activity. The departure from past practice is the venture into the social sciences.

In historical terms, economics as a separate academic discipline is quite young. The first suggestions in English that economics, as distinct from political economy, had a distinctive content came in the 1870s (Jevons 1879: 1957 xiv–xv). The first *Principles of Economics* was Alfred Marshall's volume of 1890. Modern historians of the subject naturally carry its origins back much further – to the Greeks, as might be expected. But the discipline itself is quite modern.

Perhaps because of its relative newness, economics does not have a strong sense of its own history. If anything, its sense of its own past has recently been in relative decline, perhaps because economists have found their place in the sun and do not feel obliged to emphasise their lineage to the same extent. Courses in the history of economic thought do exist in many universities, but they are far from universal and they are rarely near the centre of the undergraduate or graduate curriculum. In many departments, even those with expertise in the area, graduate students are actively discouraged from undertaking dissertations on the history of thought lest they impair their chances of success in the market for jobs where technical expertise in developing the theoretical tools of the trade is at a premium. As a result, in any year the number of dissertations submitted to universities in Canada, Great Britain and the United States can be counted on one's fingers.

The emphasis on technical skills has been accompanied in economics by what one might call a crude natural-scientific attitude. Newest is best and involves all that is worth saving from the past. If it comes in at all, the past has a minor supporting role: it provides justifications in controversy for positions originally taken up on other grounds. Rarely, however, do economists reflect on the fact that they are probably less interested in their past than their natural scientist role models. But then historians of economics have not produced many studies of their subject of the quality of, say, Richard Westfall's *Never at Rest: A Biography of Isaac Newton* (1980).

A discipline relatively uninterested in its past is unlikely to place a high value on the production of editions, even of the work of its greatest figures. However, particularly as a result of the patronage of the Royal Economic Society, first supported by John Maynard Keynes and subsequently by Austin Robinson, there have been a number of outstanding editions. One need only think of Piero Sraffa's Ricardo, William Jaffé's Walras, Dennis O'Brien's Overstone and the

University of Glasgow's edition of Adam Smith. As the Conference itself indicates, there are even more editions in the works.

As in the past, these editions will be productions of one or at most two editors, often working with minimal research assistance. Although large team projects have come to other areas of economics, they have not yet reached the editorial project. Most of these editor-economists will have worked in relative isolation from their few fellows in the discipline and probably completely isolated from editors in other disciplines. For example, no economist-editor has yet attended or delivered a paper to the Society for Textual Scholarship. This isolation has frequently resulted in the editorial equivalent of re-inventing the wheel. It has, as the Conference confirmed, also led, as often happens in isolated communities, to peculiarities in the use of language. While non-economist editors clearly distinguish between an individual's letters and correspondence, reserving the former term for out-letters and the latter for both out and in-letters, economists frequently use the terms as synonyms. Non-economist editors use the term variorum for an edition containing the notes of various commentators or editors, while for economists it has come to mean an edition of variants among several versions of a given text, such as the eight editions of Marshall's *Principles of Economics* or the printed version and drafts of Keynes's *General Theory of Employment, Interest and Money*. However, peculiarities of language should not obscure similarities in editorial problems.

This Conference represented an attempt to reduce the relative isolation of economist editors from each other and from the normal editorial clientele for such meetings. To make the encounter more tractable, the emphasis was on the work of economists after 1870. We thus excluded Smith, Ricardo, Bentham, Malthus, Marx and the Mills, all of whom have been subjects of editions completed in the last 35 years or in progress. Within the period chosen, we then tried to get examples of all the relevant types of available materials – books, professional papers, diaries, letters, correspondence, policy papers both public and official and lecture notes. The result is the present volume.

In it is a substantial accumulation of editorial experience – no fewer than 44 volumes completed or in progress. The materials dealt with cover the full range of those available to most editors of late nineteenth and twentieth century figures. Despite the similarities in raw materials some differences emerged. Inevitably we got at least one economist's model of the ideal edition from Bob Black. Also all the editors, perhaps because of their disciplinary base, again and again emphasised the role of editorial constraints. Not surprisingly, one was money. Even within the relatively spacious confines of the 30 volume Keynes edition this meant limited space. This brought problems of selection to the fore and, in the case of Tom Rymes's student notes of Keynes's lectures, a novel approach to the production of a final text. Problems of selection and treatment were on occasion heightened by the sheer volume of material extant. Carbon copies, even in the absence of acid-free paper, increase the probability of survival of any modern editor's raw materials, but economist-editors, with possible concerns with their subjects' involvement in the formulation of economic policy, also have to cope with the results of the paper-preserving proclivities of modern bureaucracies. The rules of thumb for selecting for publication from the material available – and they are rules of thumb – varied. Major articles in academic journals deemed important to the discipline, those versions of unpublished policy papers an author chose to take with him on leaving Government service, the importance in some sense of the issues under discussion, the favouring of professional over personal, all emerged as criteria. To some extent the criteria adopted were a reflection of the intended audience. Inevitably, economists edit for historians of economics or economists, but most editors also had a non-professional economist audience in mind, particularly historians, other social scientists and philosophers of science.

Prospective audiences shape economists' editions in another fashion. The annotation deemed necessary by an editor is to some extent a function of the intended audience. The more varied the audience, the more extensive the task. Surprisingly, however, in most of the papers where the issue was raised there was a certain timelessness to the principle. As the past recedes, and it is unlikely that any of the editions under discussion will be done again for several generations – if at all – it is inevitable that what one assumes as common knowledge amongst specialists now will not be the case for our successors. Thus it is far from clear that the target audience principle, which may tend towards editorial minimalism, is really all that helpful as an editorial principle.

The alternative principle of diminishing returns, also raised at the Conference, constrains editors as well, especially when it is coupled with John Whitaker's principle of increasingly likely editorial incompetence as the editor moves further away from his own area of scholarly expertise. With constraints of time and money, elaborate or exhaustive annotation may not be efficient. The same principle of diminishing returns and the same temporal and financial constraints also appear in some papers as eventually limiting the search for one's original editorial raw materials, although all would acknowledge that the often serendipitous way in which materials survive and come to rest in particular hands means that the unexpected significant find is almost inevitable – often after publication.

An emphasis on constraints, efficiency and diminishing returns in a discussion by economists is not all that surprising. All these notions will offend editorial purists. The notions may be more tangible to the single scholar-editor. Yet even with much larger scale enterprises the same problems exist: resources are not infinite even when foundations or government granting councils are involved. Thus although our economist-editors' concerns, especially as discussed in their own tribal language, may sound parochial, they do raise an issue not always sufficiently appreciated elsewhere. All editorial enterprises are constrained. Perhaps a greater awareness of these constraints at the outset would improve our design of our own projects and, perhaps, even their execution.

The annual Conference depends on several people and institutions for its success. Support to run the Conference and publish the proceedings came from the Social Sciences and Humanities Research Council of Canada, the Royal Economic Society, University College, the Department of Economics and the Office of the President, University of Toronto, and AMS Press. The School of Graduate Studies provided needed logistical support. The labours of the convener were eased by his colleagues on the Conference's Executive Committee, in particular Jerry Bentley, the Chairman, who was always available when needed with wise advice; John Grant, who ensured that local arrangements were perfect; Michael Gervers who handled the publicity to tap an audience previously unknown to the Committee; and Richard Landon who had been there last year and knew what might go wrong. During the Conference itself Catherine Schenk, praised in the pages that follow as a research assistant, provided the skills and dependability to ease things along smoothly. Finally, George Stigler, who was in Toronto for another purpose, agreed to address the delegates after dinner on Friday evening on his views as a consumer of economists' editions over many years. He thus became the first Nobel Laureate to address the Conference. His usual clear-headedness and sharpness certainly stimulated discussion. To all of the above, and to my fellow contributors, I offer a heartfelt thanks.

Works Cited

Jevons, W. Stanley 1879: 1957, *The Principles of Political Economy*, 5th edition, New York: Augustus M. Kelley.

Westfall, R. 1980, *Never at Rest: A Biography of Isaac Newton*, Cambridge: Cambridge University Press.

Editing the Papers of W.S. Jevons

R.D. Collison Black

Introduction

Since through the accidents of chronology it falls to me to give the first paper at this conference, the task of placing this and other papers in context falls to me also.

Many of the earlier conferences in this series have dealt with the problems of editing a particular type of material, for example, sixteenth century texts. Now such texts might involve the work of various classes of author – poets, playwrights and so on. In this conference, as in some others recently, we are concerned with the problems of editing a specific class of authors, economists, who may have produced a variety of types of material – published books and contributions to journals, official reports and memoranda, unpublished manuscripts, lecture notes and correspondence.

Let us begin from the most obvious and basic question –

why should material of this kind be subjected to the process of editing at all? Presumably because that process will either tend to clarify and improve understanding of the contribution which the economist in question made to his discipline or make available contributions by that economist which were not previously known to exist, or at least were not generally available. It could be said, although rather broadly and imprecisely, that the first of these results might follow from new editions of works previously published, the second from editing unpublished material.

The audience for work of this kind will consist mainly, though not entirely, of members of the economics profession. Herein lies the source of most of the special problems involved in editing economists – a statement which is not quite so obvious and banal as it might seem. Economists are, or at least like to consider themselves as, scientists engaged in the observation and analysis of the economic system. Editing, on the other hand, is a form or aspect of literary scholarship; as such, it is a type of intellectual activity about which the great majority of modern economists know little and care less, because they do not see it as relevant to their science.

It is for this reason that editions of economists' works which incorporate a full scale textual apparatus are comparatively rare. What J.M. Robson said of philosophers in his contribution to the second of this series of conferences twenty years ago remains true of economists today – "Most philosophers...would find nothing disturbing and little of interest in being told that the very widely used Everyman edition of [J.S. Mill's] *Utilitarianism* is a reprint from the first edition, with some normalization of spelling and punctuation, a few typographical errors, and no indication of which edition it represents."

As Robson added, "from the standpoint of the serious (i.e., bibliographically oriented) literary scholar, such an attitude is archaic, diseased, and generally pernicious" (Robson

1967, 111); but, for the reasons already given, economists are unlikely to be concerned about that either. Moreover, insofar as they take any interest in the writings of their predecessors, the texts in which they are mainly interested are perhaps most frequently of the nineteenth and twentieth centuries, and even in the literary field this "remains the period where critics have been least interested in textual concerns" (Bowers 1966, 35). It is generally only those variations in text between editions which reveal significant changes in the thinking of the economist-author which interest the economist-reader, and some members of the profession have expressed heretical doubts about the value of the elaborate apparatus deployed in variorum editions (Stigler 1962, 285; Bladen 1962, 1129).

The reaction of the economics audience to the editing of hitherto unpublished material by distinguished past members of their profession is likely to be somewhat similar. If the material contains original contributions to the discipline by the author, or casts fresh light on contributions previously published by that author, then naturally the interest of the audience is assured. The same may be said of material consisting of papers or memoranda written on government service or submitted to official bodies which provide new insights into the part played by the author in making policy, and into the ideas used in that process.

The unpublished papers of an economist may, however, include much which falls outside these guidelines. Personal diaries, notebooks and correspondence are likely to provide the largest category of such material. Anyone charged with the task of editing the papers of an eminent literary or political personage would probably have no hesitation in deciding that as much as possible of writings like these should be included in their published volumes. Yet those who have undertaken to edit the papers of economists have generally defined the purpose of their edition as being to show the chosen author "as an economist" or "as a working economist" (cf Keynes

1971, I: viii; Jaffé 1965a, I: vii) – and this raises the question of how far biographical material is germane to that purpose. The whole question of the relation between biographical information and the study of the development of economics as a science has been the subject of some controversy. George Stigler has argued that "those parts of a man's life which do not affect the relationships between that man and his fellow-scientists are simply extra-scientific. When we are told that we must study a man's life to understand what he really meant, we are being invited to abandon science" (1976, 60; 1982, 91). The late William Jaffé, on the other hand, always maintained that the original contributions of an individual economist cannot be properly understood without reference to his particular character and circumstances as revealed by his biography (Jaffé, 1965b, 227). These diametrically opposed views have both come under criticism as being too extreme, and recently Donald Walker has sought to bring out more clearly the ways in which biography may or may not be useful in the study of the development of economic thought with the aid of a classificatory framework. In this, biographical information about a writer can be separated into *personal*, *professional*, *environmental* and *bibliographic* categories. According to Walker,

> the genesis of a writer's idea or theory is in principle explicable by his biography, including his knowledge of the character and problems of his discipline. The role of his ideas in the evolution of the discipline, however, can be fully described without reference to his biography. The sociology of the discipline in regard to a writer's ideas can help to explain the speed with which they were adopted, and the answers to many sociological questions about the discipline involve biographical information. It is not necessary to study a writer's personal or professional biography to understand the

meaning of his ideas, nor therefore to judge their value. Knowledge of a writer's sources can be of value for establishing the meaning of his ideas and therefore for evaluating their scientific worth, and insofar as biographical research uncovers those sources it is of indirect value for those purposes. Biographical environmental information may reveal social, economic, and political influences on a writer, and in some cases may help to explain his meaning. (Walker 1983, 57–8)

Walker's scheme may prove helpful to future editors in deciding whether to include or exclude letters or papers giving personal and professional information about their "editee", but his treatment of the subject makes clear that in the case of economists the decision is seldom likely to be simple and clear cut.

These are some of the main respects in which the task of editing the collected works, or even the papers and correspondence, of an economist seems to me to differ from editing, say, the sonnets of Shakespeare or the correspondence of Madame de Sévigné. It follows that it is a task which can usually only be undertaken by a professional economist – yet if one accepts their own theories it would seem that no economist should undertake it. If economists are rational maximisers whose decisions are always the result of conscious and fully informed weighing of alternatives one would not expect to find them allocating time to editing the published or unpublished work of their predecessors. For the economist who does this is not only committing himself to a considerable amount of work over a considerable period of time, but giving himself the duty of seeking to acquire some command of another discipline, and one which is not highly marketable within his own profession. Even if his research yields important results, such, say, as the re-discovery of a neglected theory, it has recently been argued that "investment in research which produces output in the form of a novel theory or application generates a gain to society which is fully (or at least more fully) internalized by the investor than investment in research which produces output in the form of a re-discovery of a generally neglected earlier theory or applications, *ceteris paribus*" (Anderson and Tollison 1986, 63).

If it is indeed the case that "research investment in the history of thought will tend to generate a larger margin of external benefits than research in economics generally" (ibid.), then it is clear that only a minority of economists will undertake it, and within that minority fewer still are likely to engage in editing texts and documents rather than commenting upon them. Who will form the members of this sub-set, this eccentric minority within a minority? They need not necessarily be irrational people, but only people who feel that there is a place for scholarship within economics and in whose utility function the production of scholarly results bulks fairly large.

"I give", said Jacob Viner, "only an old-fashioned and modest meaning to the term 'scholarship'. I mean by it nothing more than the pursuit of broad and exact knowledge of the history of the working of the human mind as revealed in written records" (Viner 1950: 1958, 369). To contribute to that knowledge, to make it both broader and more exact, is the true *raison d'etre* of editions of economists, and their significance must be measured in terms of their effects on subsequent work in the area. No one writes, or could write, now about Ricardo without reference to the material which Piero Sraffa made available in his edition of Ricardo's *Works and Correspondence*. No one writes, or could write, now about Walras, without reference to the *Correspondence and Related Papers* on which Bill Jaffé lavished so many years of meticulous research. Every economist-editor can live and work in the hope that the same may come to be said of his or her volumes, and look for reward mainly in the footnotes and reference lists of other people's writings.

Editing Jevons: General Principles

In the preceding section I have tried to provide a rationale for editing economists. Yet in my own case I have to admit that it might be more accurately and honestly described as an *ex post* rationalisation, and I suspect I am not alone in this. For an edition of the works and papers of a leading economist is perhaps not so much something which people are likely deliberately and advisedly to decide to do as to have happen to them.

In support of this view, I may cite the "three golden rules for editing large-scale correspondences" laid down by Ralph Leigh in his paper on Rousseau's Correspondence, presented to the fourteenth of these conferences in 1978. They are:

1. Be rich, and, if possible, influential too.
2. Be young and vigorous, and make up your mind never to grow old.
3. Always start at least a hundred years before you actually do. (Leigh 1979, 42)

Anyone who has edited an economist's papers, including or excluding correspondence, will recognise that these rules are valid, but will surely also echo Professor Leigh's rueful comment – "I'm afraid I have broken all these rules." Certainly that has been my experience in editing the papers of William Stanley Jevons. Had it been made clear to me at the outset that these were the golden rules of the job I was undertaking, I should probably never have started, and I expect most editors of economists would say the same. Mercifully it does not become starkly clear until you are well embarked on the task, by which time you already are interested and are developing a vested interest in it yourself; it has happened to you.

The process whereby editing the papers of W.S. Jevons

happened to me is outlined in the Preface to Volume I of *Papers and Correspondence of W.S. Jevons* (Black 1972–81, hereafter referred to as *P & C*) and I need not restate it here. It may, however, be useful for me to recapitulate the major editorial decisions which faced me at the outset.

The first arose from the fact that there had been a considerable amount of previous editorial work on the Jevons papers, undertaken after his death in 1882 by his widow, Harriet A. Jevons, with the help of such distinguished contemporaries as H.S. Foxwell, Henry Higgs, Philip Wicksteed and F.Y. Edgeworth. This process has recently been the subject of an excellent paper by Jevons's grand-daughter, Mrs. Rosamond Könekamp (1982). As she there explains, Jevons in 1882 was engaged in collecting most of his published and unpublished papers into two volumes. One, containing an assortment of papers on labour and social issues was edited with only a brief preface by Mrs. Jevons herself and appeared in 1883 under the title *Methods of Social Reform*. The other, comprising his monetary writings, was edited by Foxwell and published as *Investigations in Currency and Finance* in 1884.

Of the several books which Jevons had in plan or in progress when he died, only one was sufficiently far advanced to allow of its publication, and then only in part. This was the "very novel and complete treatise on Political Economy" which he had started upon in October 1880 (*P & C*, V, 110). After many delays this appeared as *Principles of Economics* in 1903, edited by Henry Higgs, in a volume which also included another four of Jevons's papers (three published and one unpublished) which had escaped the earlier collections.

Since good reprints of these and all the other books on economics which Jevons wrote were, and still are, readily obtainable it seemed, and still seems, clear to me that to produce a completely new edition of the collected economic writings of W.S. Jevons would not be a practical proposition. New editions of his books to modern standards could no doubt incorporate many improvements, but these would be marginal rather than substantial and in view of the attitude of most economists to editorial refinements it is evident that such new editions simply would not find a market.

Nevertheless, even after deducting all this work from the scope of a possible new edition, there remained much material in the Jevons Papers which either had not been published at all or which could benefit significantly from new editing. There were a number of papers, both published and unpublished, which had somehow not been included in the collected volumes, and there was a complete set of notes of a course of lectures delivered by Jevons in 1875–6, copied out and sent to him by one of his students, which had only barely been mentioned in *Letters and Journal* (Jevons 1886, 383). What emerged most clearly perhaps was that those very letters and journal which Mrs. Jevons had used as the basis of her 1886 book had been handled by her in a manner which would not meet modern standards of editing at all. In all fairness it deserves to be emphasised that her objective was not to produce an edition of her husband's letters and journals which would satisfy even the standards of 1886, but to tell the story of his life by means of extracts from them connected by short passages of explanatory narrative.

In seeking to achieve that objective, Mrs. Jevons made a selection from the letters available to her, omitting many entirely and deleting from others passages which she deemed unimportant or capable of giving offence to persons then living. Similarly she made extracts from Jevons's journals, omitting many of the highly personal passages in which he referred to family matters or revealed his own emotions. Again, as was appropriate to a narrative, Harriet Jevons did not seek to interrupt its flow by detailed notes and references documenting the people and events which came into it.

Hence it seemed to me that there was scope for an edition of these papers which would make them available to students of the history of ideas in full and fully referenced, notwithstanding the fact that the earlier editing had ensured that, as I wrote in 1970, "it cannot be claimed that either the letters or the papers contain theories or ideas of major significance which have never previously been published" (*P & C*, I, xii). For, to adopt Walker's terminology, they did contain much environmental and bibliographic as well as more strictly personal and professional information which could contribute to our understanding of Jevons's life and work.

Once it had been decided that for these reasons an edition of the papers and correspondence of W.S. Jevons should be undertaken, another decision of general editorial principle had then to be taken. The papers remaining could be divided into two broad categories, personal and professional, with the latter again sub-dividing into those related to economics and those related to logic. To edit the logical papers of W.S. Jevons required the expertise of a logician, and that work had already been begun by Dr. Wolfe Mays of the Department of Philosophy, University of Manchester. It was clearly appropriate that he should continue it and similarly Mrs. Könekamp's unrivalled knowledge of the Jevons family papers and history seemed to make it obvious that she should edit the personal letters and journals, leaving only the strictly economic papers to be dealt with by me. "Unfortunately, towards the end of 1968, when the editing of both parts of the papers was well advanced, Mrs. Könekamp found that her state of health would not permit her to continue with the work" (*P & C*, I, xi), although fortunately she remained willing to help with advice, of which indeed she has been a vitally important and much valued source throughout the work. These circumstances led to the final division of editorial responsibilities being somewhat different from what I had intended, with the scope of my own task extending beyond the purely economic material.

Before this occurred Mrs. Könekamp had written an

important Biographical Introduction which provides the background for the whole edition, and finished the editing of the complete text of her grandfather's personal journal, which constitutes the most important single addition to the sources available for the study of his life. There remained, however, a considerable volume of personal correspondence on which I had to make the decision whether to include or exclude.

Looking to other more experienced editors for guidance on this point produces conflicting evidence. C.R. Sanders, the editor of Carlyle's letters, argues persuasively that "there can be only one logical answer to our question. All snippets must be published and all long letters published in their entirety for indexing and for biographers and other scholars who may want to use the letters as source material" (Sanders 1967, 86). On the other hand "Professor Mineka urges the wisdom of merely listing notes accepting, declining, or offering invitations to dine, etc." says John M. Robson, who himself characterises such trivia as "weeds amid the glorious blossoms" (Robson 1967, 99).

I tend to share the latter view and in deciding whether to include or exclude a personal letter I used two criteria – that to justify inclusion it should either throw light on the development of Jevons's ideas or provide some insights into the economic and social history of his time. I would be prepared to argue that these are reasonable criteria to apply in the case of an economist whose fame has resulted primarily from his original ideas, but who in his applied work was not uninfluenced by, or without influence upon, the circumstances and conditions of his time. They are also criteria designed to meet the needs of a wider audience than purely professional economists – historians and sociologists of science, for example.

From these broader issues of editorial principle I turn now to consider more specific and detailed editorial problems. Following the usual convention, I shall divide these into (i) purely textual problems and (ii) problems of annotation and interpretation, but adding a third, perhaps a typical economist's category, (iii) problems of production and finance.

Textual Problems

There are textual problems with every type of material, especially manuscript material, but in the Jevons Papers the most numerous and difficult ones arose with letters; and the problems of gathering together the texts exceeded those of establishing the text once obtained. To edit letters usefully it is clearly desirable to have both sides of the correspondence in full, for "without the correspondents' replies, the reader is like a person hearing only one side of a telephone conversation" (Lewis 1979, 30), but in the case of Jevons this basic *desideratum* was for the most part not satisfied.

Writing a little before the period when typewriters came into general use, Jevons did not keep any copies of his letters; nor did he make a preliminary draft of a letter, unless it was of quite exceptional significance to him. Consequently, what survived in his papers were almost entirely letters received by him. An initial problem, therefore, was to establish the whereabouts of letters *from* Jevons. Announcements were made in the *Economic Journal*, *The Manchester School*, and other publications requesting information on this point. These, combined with personal enquiries, at first produced details of a number of small but significant groups of Jevons letters, notably those in the Fonds Walras at Lausanne and in the Palgrave Papers at King's College, Cambridge. But after these initial successes extended enquiries yielded sharply diminishing returns. One difficulty in those days was to discover both the existence and the whereabouts of economists' papers in which letters might be found; that problem has been greatly reduced, in Britain at least, by the sterling work of Paul Sturges in compiling a guide to archive sources for our subject (Sturges 1975).

That extended searches should yield diminishing returns will hardly surprise any economist, but unfortunately the field of manuscript sources does not correspond with the assumptions of Ricardian rent theory. The most fertile soil is not always that which is first cultivated and one never can be sure, so long as significant parts of the total correspondence remain unlocated, that one may not "strike it rich" at the next attempt.

This raises the awkward question of when to stop searching and start publishing. Editing economists involves, as the recorded instances demonstrate, a very extended period of production but it cannot be infinite. At some point the editor must deliver his typescript to the printer, trusting that he will not be presented with the mixed blessing of a rich discovery of hitherto untraced letters while it is in the press, or, worse still, some time after publication. I have had one or two such disconcerting experiences, which I have detailed elsewhere (Black 1982). Here let me just recall that the discovery of a number of Jevons's letters among the Foxwell Papers, which Mr. R.D. Freeman kindly made available to me, came in time to allow them to be annotated and published in *P & C*, but too late to permit the re-numbering of all the correspondence in proper sequence without disturbing the cross-references in volumes already published.

I had less luck with Jevons's letters to his younger brother Thomas Edwin (Tom) which came to my attention only in 1982, the year after the last volume in my series had been published. They formed part of a collection now known as the Seton-Jevons Papers, and preserved in the archives of Seton Hall University, South Orange, New Jersey. This particular case illustrates another peculiar difficulty which faces the searcher for letters and papers – even when he does locate the owner of a collection that owner may prove unwilling to give him access to it, or even to be unaware of what he has in his possession. For the Seton-Jevons papers were discovered, after his death, in the house of Ferdinand Jevons, the youngest son of Thomas Edwin Jevons and his wife, the former Isabel Seton. A few years earlier Ferdinand Jevons had stated categorically in writing not merely to me but to Miss Winefrid Jevons, his first cousin, that he possessed no papers or letters of W.S. Jevons at all. Yet the collection proved to contain almost a hundred such letters. It must be accepted, I think, that he either never knew of, or had entirely forgotten about, their existence.

In the particular case of the Jevons Papers there was also the problem that quite a few letters which were no longer in the collection and could not be traced had been published, in part at least, by Harriet Jevons in *Letters and Journal*. We know that when compiling it she had written to as many of her late husband's correspondents as she could trace, asking them to lend her any of his letters which they might have. Those she received she copied and returned, but many of these were lost either in that process or subsequently. Here Lewis's first rule – "Do what is Best for the Reader" (Lewis 1979, 33) – clearly indicated that whatever part of the letter had been printed in Jevons (1886) should be reprinted in *P & C*, with an appropriate symbol to indicate the source. In the case where the original manuscript of a letter, from which extracts were printed in Jevons (1886), had survived, the full text was included in *P & C*, again with an indication that some parts had been published in the earlier volume.

I would argue that when an editor has the previously published version of a letter but cannot trace the original manuscript, he does better to publish that version rather than nothing at all. Yet clearly there are dangers in the process, as is well illustrated by the case of Jevons's letter to Walras of 12 May 1874. This had been published by Mrs. Jevons (1886, 302–4) in a version which contains a number of obvious mistakes, corrected by Jaffé in his edition of the Walras Correspondence (1965a 1: 393–5). In the absence of the original manuscript this seemed to be the best interpretation of the text possible, and I followed it in *P & C*, IV, 39–41. Arnold Heertje rediscovered the missing manuscript in 1981, and was thus able to publish for the first time a text which is completely faithful to the original. Not surprisingly, perhaps, several minor differences from Jaffé's corrected text appear in it; but the major difference is that one evident mistake in the version published by Mrs. Jevons, and corrected by Jaffé, appears in the original manuscript: Jevons had made a slip in writing out his own equations! Part of the text which appeared in Jevons (1886) does, as Jaffé said, make evident nonsense; but the revelation that Jevons's own autograph letter contained a slip in turn makes nonsense of my attempt, in a learned footnote, to provide a rational explanation of how the general confusion might have come about (cf Heertje 1982, 412–16).

Interpretation and Annotation

Once possessed of a text, the editor's next tasks are those of interpreting and annotating it, and his duty is to be at one and the same time as helpful and as unobtrusive as possible – two roles which are not always easily reconcilable.

In interpretation, as I see it, the aim must be to put the reader of the printed published text as nearly as possible in the same position as if he were reading the original manuscript, only sorting out for him those points which might interfere with his ability to appreciate its full meaning at one reading. Subject to this over-riding principle my view is that the text should be reproduced in full, "warts and all", whatever eccentricities of spelling and grammar it may contain. To this it can be objected that it may involve peppering pages with "[*sic*]"; but so far as spelling is concerned I found it possible to avoid this by inserting a footnote where the first mis-spelling occurred, worded as follows:

> This is one of many idiosyncrasies of spelling which
> occur throughout the family correspondence, particu-
> larly in the letters of Thomas Jevons; all subsequent
> instances are denoted by an asterisk.

Grammatical errors arose mainly in letters from correspondents whose native language was not English and as such were
generally self-explanatory.

Diagrams and mathematical expressions can present many
problems in editing economists, even when the original text
is available. The temptation is to re-draw diagrams neatly on
modern lines, but this involves the danger of their being mod-
ified in the process in a way which obscures the author's
intentions. Following out the general principle I have outlined
above, I adopted the plan of reproducing diagrams photo-
graphically, in order to retain the character of the original as
completely as possible. Similarly with mathematics I followed
the original text exactly, using footnotes to draw attention to
any possible slips, or points requiring clarification.

Interpretation here shades over almost imperceptibly into
annotation, by far the largest and most difficult part of the
editor's work. The economist here shares the problem of all
editors of papers and correspondence in trying to steer a middle course between burdening his readers with superfluous
information and leaving them frustrated and bewildered by
his failure to identify who's who and what's what. In the
process he is likely to develop a curious set of skills somewhere
between those of a private detective and an archaeologist, a
great familiarity with obscure works of reference, and a case
of hypertension, identified by Wilmarth Lewis as almost an
occupational disease of editors (Lewis 1979, 33).

Editing Jevons afforded me many instances of the truth
of these points, but I have little doubt that every other editor

could produce a parallel set of illustrations, so I need not parade mine here. In the correspondence the principal problems were the identification of people and events which have found no place in history, and perhaps not even in the newspapers of the day, but a secondary problem was the source of unattributed quotations. Serendipity plays a surprisingly large part in the solution of such problems, along with patience and commitment, but again there is a difficulty in recognising when the investment of time should cease.

By comparison with the correspondence, the manuscript notes of Jevons's lectures on political economy given at Owens College, Manchester, in 1875–76 (*P & C*, VI) presented relatively few problems of annotation and interpretation. These notes were taken by one of his students, Harold Rylett, who made a fair copy of them about two years later and sent it to Jevons. Acknowledging Rylett's gift, Jevons himself identified the main problem with the text when he wrote: "It is interesting to read what purports to be a verbatim report, but which has, I fear, undergone some improvement in the process. It is well known how much of the oratory we read is due to the reporters" (*P & C*, IV, 241). That Rylett, who apparently took his notes mainly in longhand, was not the most accurate of verbatim reporters can be demonstrated at certain points in the notes where the argument can be checked against Jevons's published works, especially his *Theory of Political Economy*. At all such points my policy was to identify any omissions or mistakes and supply what appeared to be the correct reading in notes. At other points the solution was not always so simple. Sometimes Rylett himself could not fully reconstruct his abbreviated notes when he came to copy them out, and supplied alternative readings for a word or phrase about which he remained in doubt. Unfortunately Jevons himself, who was uniquely placed to provide the correct interpretation, appears never to have gone through the notes with this purpose in view. Again applying Lewis's first rule in such cases suggested that the editor should if possible indicate the most likely interpretation, but there remained instances in which the best course seemed to be to leave the alternative readings as Rylett had presented them and allow the reader to place his own interpretation on them.

Editor's hypertension is not eased by finding interpolations by the student such as "(There seems to have been a table on the board – or a diagram which I do not appear to have copied.)" (*P & C*, VI, 127); but fortunately in this case the context makes clear beyond doubt that the diagram was Jevons's *Diagram showing all the Weekly Accounts of the Bank of England since the passing of the Bank Act of 1844*, which was reprinted in his *Investigations in Currency and Finance*. Once provided with this key, the whole lecture could be explicated clearly in a single footnote. Indeed the fact that Jevons normally told his class very clearly what his sources were and gave full reading recommendations greatly simplified the process of annotating these lectures.

Problems of Production and Finance

Model building is the essence of modern economic theory, so it would seem appropriate to apply the technique here, endeavouring to construct a model of the editorial process. Like all simple economic models, it must be constructed by abstraction from, and idealisation of, observed reality.

From the available range of models the most appropriate to select would seem to be the familiar microeconomic-model of the demand, supply and pricing of a consumers good. A variety of assumptions might be made about the demand for the edition, but the most realistic would seem to be that it is narrowly limited and comes mainly from institutional rather than private buyers. With such a narrow market total revenue generated by sales may be insufficient to cover total costs. It is therefore necessary to make a further assumption; that the economy includes grant-giving bodies endowed either from public funds or private benefactions for cultural and educational purposes. Production of the edition then depends on making a case which these bodies will accept that it falls within their purposes to provide the necessary funds to cover the anticipated deficit.

Turning then to the process of producing the edition, the first steps would be the collection of all the materials to be edited and the securing of guarantees of all the funds, over and above expected sales revenues, necessary to finance the process through to its completion. These two stages might be undertaken simultaneously but no other steps would be taken before these vital first two were complete.

This achieved, the editor-entrepreneur should be free to devote at least half, but preferably the whole, of his time to the process of interpretation and annotation. This process is necessarily labour-intensive and time-consuming, but there are possibilities of substitution in it. These are possibilities not so much of substituting capital for labour as of substituting money for time. The more funds there are available the more, and the more expert, the research assistance which can be employed and so the more quickly can the process of editing be completed.

When, and only when, a definitive typescript of the text has been fully annotated in this way and finally completed is it delivered to the publishers, who then give first priority to the production of clean proofs. Indexing, preferably by those trained and experienced in that art, can then proceed from page proofs while the editor weeds out such few errors as these may contain. Finally then, the volumes are printed off, bound and published.

Economists who have actually got into the editing game will know that this production model for the perfect edition is as remote from reality as the familiar model of perfect competition. My own experience approximated more closely to the model at some points in the editing process than at others. Holding a university post which involved the duties of departmental Chairman (and at some times Dean or Pro-Vice-Chancellor) as well as a full teaching load, I was scarcely ever able to devote my full time to the process of editing Jevons and not often as much as half. But I was fortunate in having at my disposal most of the time of a Research Officer on the university establishment and the fact that one holder of that post, Mrs. Jacqueline Wright, worked on the Jevons edition from 1969 until after its completion in 1981 was of inestimable benefit to me. I am happy to take this occasion to express my gratitude to Mrs. Wright for her great assistance in the editing process. I was also fortunate in being able to have the complete index to the whole series of volumes compiled by Mrs. Barbara Lowe, of Cambridge (England), who prepared the index to Sraffa's edition of Ricardo and was also responsible for the indexes to all of the volumes of Keynes's *Collected Writings*. Sadly, Mrs. Lowe died in 1984; her unique contribution to the cause of editing economists should certainly receive due homage at this conference.

I was fortunate too in obtaining the financial sponsorship of the Royal Economic Society for the Jevons edition at the outset. Here, however, unforeseen developments caused reality to diverge more widely from the ideal than at most other points. The edition was originally planned in four volumes – one containing a Biographical Introduction by Mrs. Könekamp and the complete text of Jevons's personal journal, two containing correspondence and another the lectures of 1875–76 and any remaining papers, published or unpublished. By 1973 the first two volumes had been edited and published according to plan. After that two unexpected events coincided – much extra material became available in the Foxwell papers and elsewhere, and the rate of inflation began to rise with unprecedented rapidity. The resultant rise in printing costs, together with the increased bulk of material, made it impossible for the publishers to maintain the planned size and format of the remaining volumes. Volume III was split into three smaller volumes of correspondence, and Volume IV became two, one containing the lectures and the other the hitherto uncollected papers and the index to the whole set.

All this was inescapable if the edition was to be completed at all – and there were times when it seemed that financial difficulties might prevent publication of anything beyond the first two volumes. Nevertheless it had consequences which present and future readers will deplore. Volumes I and II contain cross-references to Volume III and IV which fortunately are not meaningless – because it proved possible to retain the original numbering of the letters – but still require to be interpreted with understanding. That understanding, in turn, can only be derived from reading the Preface to Volume III as well as that to Volume I.

Simple micro-models usually assume a constant price level, and when that assumption is not fulfilled it can play havoc with the whole production process. On the other hand such models normally also assume a constant technology, while in practice changing technologies can affect production and costs fundamentally.

In this respect the Jevons edition may have come at just the wrong time – in time to suffer the full effects of the inflation of the seventies, but too soon to experience the benefits of the new techniques of word processing and computerised typesetting. For if editorial scholarship has an enemy in inflation it may have a new friend in word processing, which so greatly simplifies the problems of adding, deleting or modifying text and footnotes, and in computerised typesetting itself.

Some are inclined to see in new technology a threat to scholarship, which has always been, perhaps, a slightly old fashioned craft. I venture to think that it may rather prove to be an unexpected ally if properly handled and to hope, with rather less confidence, that in years to come inflation and attempts to keep it in control may not prevent universities and research funding agencies from sometimes taking a favourable view of proposals to subject economists to editorial scholarship.

Works Cited

Anderson, Gary M. and Tollison, R.D. 1986, "Dead Men Tell No Tales", *History of Economics Society Bulletin* 8, No. 1, 59–68.

Black, R.D. Collison (ed.) 1972–81, *Papers and Correspondence of William Stanley Jevons*, Volumes I–VII, London: Macmillan in association with the Royal Economic Society.

Black, R.D. Collison 1982, "The Papers and Correspondence of William Stanley Jevons: A Supplementary Note", *The Manchester School*, 50 (December) 417–28.

Bladen, V.W. 1962, Review of *Principles of Economics* by Alfred Marshall. Ninth (Variorum) Edition with annotations by C.W. Guillebaud, *American Economic Review*, 52 (December), 1127–9.

Bowers, Fredson 1966, "Old Wine in New Bottles: Problems of Machine Printing" in Robson, J.M. (ed.), *Editing Nineteenth Century Texts*, Toronto: University of Toronto Press, 9–36.

Heertje, Arnold 1982, "An Important Letter from W.S. Jevons to L. Walras", *The Manchester School*, 50 (December), 412–16.

Jaffé, William (ed.) 1965a, *Correspondence of Léon Walras and Related Papers*, Vols. I–III, Amsterdam: North-Holland Publishing Company.

Jaffé, William 1965b, "Biography and Economic Analysis", *Western Economic Journal* III (Summer), 223–32.

Jevons, Harriet A. 1886, *Letters and Journal of W. Stanley Jevons*, Edited by his wife, London: Macmillan & Co.

Keynes, John Maynard 1971, *The Collected Writings of John Maynard Keynes*, Vol. I, *Indian Currency and Finance*, including General Introduction, London: Macmillan for the Royal Economic Society.

Könekamp, Rosamond 1982, "The Work of Harriet Ann Jevons (1838–1910) after her husband's death", *The Manchester School*, 50 (December) 379–411.

Leigh, Ralph A. 1979, "Rousseau's Correspondence: Editorial Problems", in Dainard, J.A. (ed.), *Editing Correspondence*, New York: Garland, 39–62.

Lewis, Wilmarth S. 1979, "Editing Familiar Letters", in Dainard, J.A. (ed.), *Editing Correspondence*, New York: Garland, pp. 25–38.

Robson, John M. 1967, "Principles and Methods in the Collected Works of John Stuart Mill", in Robson, J.M. (ed.), *Editing Nineteenth*

Century Texts, Toronto: University of Toronto Press, 96–122.

Sanders, Charles R. 1967, "Editing the Carlyle Letters: Problems and Opportunities", in Robson, J.M. (ed.), *Editing Nineteenth Century Texts*, Toronto: University of Toronto Press, 77–95.

Stigler, G.J. 1962, "Marshall's *Principles* after Guillebaud", *Journal of Political Economy*, 70 (November), 282–6.

— 1976:1982, "The Scientific Uses of Scientific Biography, with special reference to J.S. Mill", in Robson, J.M. and M. Laine (eds.), *James and John Stuart Mill: Papers of the Centenary Conference*, Toronto: University of Toronto Press, 55–66. Reprinted in *The Economist as Preacher*, Oxford: Blackwell, 86–97.

Sturges, R.P. 1975, *Economists' Papers 1750–1950: A Guide to Archive and other Manuscript Sources for the History of British and Irish Economic Thought*, Durham: Duke University Press.

Viner, Jacob 1950:1958, "A Modest Proposal for some Stress on Scholarship in Graduate Training", *Brown University Papers*, XXIV, reprinted in *The Long View and the Short*, Glencoe: Free Press; 369–81.

Walker, Donald A. 1983, "Biography and the Study of the History of Economic Thought", *Research in the History of Economic Thought and Methodology*, I, 41–59.

Editing Alfred Marshall

John K. Whitaker

Alfred Marshall is well known to economists but may need a brief introduction to non-economists. He was born in London in 1842 and died in Cambridge in 1924. In 1865 he was elected to a Fellowship at St. John's College, Cambridge, after becoming Second Wrangler in Cambridge University's Mathematical Tripos. The remainder of his life was spent in Cambridge, apart from an exile from 1877 to 1885 in Bristol and Oxford due to marriage to Mary Paley, an early Newnham student, which required him to resign his Cambridge Fellowship. He returned to Cambridge in 1885 as Professor of Political Economy, succeeding Henry Fawcett, and held the chair until voluntary retirement in 1908. Marshall was the founder of the Cambridge School of Economics which rose to great eminence in the inter-war period. Arthur Cecil Pigou, Marshall's successor in the Cambridge chair, and John Maynard Keynes were his most notable pupils. Marshall's masterpiece, his *Principles of Economics*, was first published in 1890 and went through eight editions during his lifetime. It was the most influential economic treatise of its era and might be said to have been the Bible of British economics for some 40 years. A ninth, variorum, two-volume edition of the *Principles* appeared in 1961, prepared by Marshall's nephew Claude W. Guillebaud, himself a Cambridge economist. Late in life, Marshall produced two more large works: *Industry and Trade* which appeared in 1919 and *Money Credit and Commerce* which appeared in 1923. Much earlier, in 1879, he had published, jointly with Mary Paley Marshall, a small book, the *Economics of Industry*, ostensibly a primer but in fact a first statement of his theoretical views. This was replaced in 1892 by Marshall's *Elements of the Economics of Industry*, essentially an abridgement of the *Principles*. Marshall's occasional publications and some of his correspondence were collected in 1925 in a volume entitled *Memorials of Alfred Marshall*, edited by Pigou, while his responses to government enquiries were collected in 1926 in a volume entitled *Official Papers of Alfred Marshall*, edited by Maynard Keynes. More recently, in 1975, I edited Marshall's early manuscripts in a two-volume work *The Early Economic Writings of Alfred Marshall, 1867–1890*. I am currently at work on an edition of Marshall's correspondence.[1]

Marshall presents the editor with three distinct problem areas: correspondence, unpublished manuscripts, and published texts. My direct involvement has been with the first two areas: in the third I have been rather a consumer than a

1/ All the books mentioned in this paragraph were published in London by Macmillan. A comprehensive list of Marshall's publications is given in *Memorials*, pp. 500–8. The famous memoir of Marshall by Maynard Keynes is to be found in *Memorials* pp. 1–65, or in any edition of Keynes's *Essays in Biography*.

producer of editorial work. Nevertheless, it seems appropriate to comment on the problems arising in all three areas and I will take them in the order listed.

I

There is ample precedent for editing the correspondence of economists. To name just a few examples, there are now excellent editions of the correspondence of Adam Smith, David Ricardo, John Stuart Mill, Léon Walras, William Stanley Jevons, and Vilfredo Pareto, all major figures in the subject. Publication of Marshall's correspondence commenced very early, a selection of about 125 pages appearing in the *Memorials* volume within a year of his death. These letters have proved a very important source of insight into Marshall's views and attitudes, and many passages have been quoted so frequently as to have become hackneyed. Since 1925 various additional letters or groups of letters have been reproduced wholly or in part in a quite unsystematic way. But a comprehensive edition, or even inventory, has been lacking. Lord Robbins (1977) termed such an edition an "essential desideratum" and it does seem the most important gap waiting to be filled in giving scholars ready access to primary material on Marshall. Marshall's letters are significant because he often expresses his opinions in a more direct and forceful way than he permitted himself in his polished, indeed over-polished, publications. This element of ease and vigor is notable even in letters written for the press. His private letters also give useful insight into his habits of thought and work and his complex personality.

Some four years ago I embarked on a systematic collection of the surviving correspondence knowing (or thinking I knew) the whereabouts of most of the material, having consulted it over the years in a desultory way. With the over-optimism characteristic of editors, and perhaps required to induce them to take on the job in the first place, I had hoped to be more or less finished by now. In fact there still remains about a year's work.

The process of preparing an edition of correspondence falls into three distinct phases – collection, selection, and presentation. Each phase involves its distinctive problems. Collection becomes relatively trivial if there is a central archive in which copies of both "out" letters by the central figure and "in" letters to the central figure are preserved (as in the cases of Léon Walras or Maynard Keynes). Unfortunately this is far from being so in Marshall's case. He did not preserve letters received in a systematic way, nor, except in a few cases, did he preserve copies of the letters he wrote. No family letters seem to have survived, apart from a small group Marshall wrote to his mother while visiting North America in the summer of 1875. About 150 "in" letters of a professional nature are preserved in the Marshall papers, now deposited in the Marshall Library, Cambridge. Many of these are formal, such as notes of thanks for a copy of one of Marshall's works. A few other "in" letters, or copies of them, have been preserved, usually by the sender, and a few were published in the *Memorials*. But coverage is evidently quite fragmentary and in most cases the "in" letters corresponding to surviving "out" letters are unavailable. The main supply of significant letters comes from "out" letters written by Marshall and preserved by the recipients. About 250 of these are now collected in the Marshall Library, the most important being those kept by two of Marshall's early students, Herbert Somerton Foxwell and John Neville Keynes (father of Maynard Keynes). About 300 further manuscript letters have come to light in various collections around the world. In addition there are letters Marshall wrote for publication which survive in printed form. There are also private letters which have previously been reproduced or quoted in print, but the originals of which can no longer be traced. This is the case for many of the letters reproduced in *Memorials*. Finally, there are a few letters to or from Mary Paley Marshall which might be construed as sent jointly to or from husband and wife.

In sum, the order of magnitude of the available stocks of letters is some 700 "out" letters and some 180 "in" letters. A good two-thirds of the "out" letters come from the period following the publication of the *Principles* in 1890, when Marshall was already 48 years old. Most of the "in" letters are post-1900. The more famous Marshall became, the more likely were his letters to be preserved by recipients, while his tendency to preserve letters received seems to have increased with age, perhaps more by default than design.

The surviving correspondence is predominantly professional in nature. Besides Foxwell and Neville Keynes, other important correspondents include Maynard Keynes, Francis Ysidro Edgeworth, Edwin Cannan, Benjamin Jowett, William Albert Samuel Hewins, Charles Ryle Fay, and the publishers Macmillan and Company in Britain; John Bates Clark, Edwin Robert Anderson Seligman, Henry Ludwell Moore, Frank William Taussig and Simon Newcomb in North America; Johan Gustav Knut Wicksell, Karl Gustav Cassel, and Ludwig Joseph (Lujo) Brentano on the Continent. In addition to the correspondences with all these, there are also scattered letters to a wide range of individuals and institutions.

A few words on the search process may be in order. Tracing letters as scattered as those of Marshall proved to be no mean task. The first step is to attempt to locate the papers of known or likely correspondents. There are some obvious aids here. The most important are Paul Sturges' (1975) guide to the papers of British economists, the National Register of Archives in London (which must be visited in person) and the *National Union Catalog of Manuscript Collections* for the U.S.A. These general aids, and similar general reference sources, can be supplemented by fragments of knowledge gleaned by personal enquiry or from footnote references in pertinent scholarly works. A remaining resort is to attempt to predict the likely locations of papers which might exist, but of which no mention has been stumbled upon. Having drawn up a list (to some extent a wish list) of likely locations, the next step is to visit them or write to the relevant archivists or possible private holders. I regard it as unreasonable to impose costs on others in cases where there is no *prima facie* reason for thinking anything could result and so avoided an entirely scatter-gun approach of indiscriminate enquiries. Even so, I made close to 100 enquiries, of which 40 or so yielded positive results. Of the latter, only three sources are in private hands. For the most part contacts have been with librarians and archivists who have almost all been helpful and cooperative. Ideally, every collection should be visited in person and the materials inspected *in situ*. But this is a counsel of perfection. In most cases xerox copies seem to be adequate – surely the xerox machine has revolutionised the editor's job more than any other single change. Of course, this leaves one very much in the hands of archivists and their finding aids, but this is true even when visiting an archive in person. It is rare to be given sufficient freedom, and have sufficient time, for unlimited rummaging around in all relevant collections.

At some point active search has to be ended. This does not mean failing to follow up new clues as they arise. But there comes a point when all known leads of any degree of credibility have been exhausted. Beyond this point search would be essentially blind. By ceasing to search before all conceivable possibilities have been fully explored one is almost ensuring that some relevant material will prove to have been missed. Yet the cost in time, effort and money of ensuring that this will not be so is prohibitive. Absolute certainty can never be achieved. As an economist I am particularly aware that it cannot be optimal in a world of scarce time and resources to search until the probability of finding new material falls to zero. The hope is that one stops when no major hoards of significant matter remain undiscovered and that any items missed are of marginal importance. But one has to live with the threat that such a hope may be dashed. Indeed, the very act of publishing an edition is likely to bring overlooked material to light. Often it is only then that those with the necessary information are made aware of its value and have an incentive to communicate their knowledge. The awareness that despite one's best efforts one may end up looking foolish, if not careless, is one of those crosses the editor must learn to bear.

Having ceased active search, the next question is that of selecting from the accumulated stock of material that portion which deserves to be reproduced. This is the stage I am at now. Three distinct constraints come to bear at this point. The first might be called the aesthetic constraint. Without wishing to argue for the kind of latitude nineteenth-century editors permitted themselves, I would urge that a collection of letters is usually improved by the exercise of a degree of selectivity. While the over-riding aim should be to provide scholars with all *important* primary material, an edition of letters or correspondence can frequently do more than this. It can convey, with an immediacy which brings dead voices back to life, a picture of the protagonist's developing biography, personality, intellectual vision, and relations with others. Ideally it should be possible to read through such a collection in sequence with both pleasure and profit. Burdening the text down with a large amount of trivial or repetitive material would threaten this kind of artistic unity even if parsimony was not called for by the second constraint, the economic one. Printing and publication are expensive. Scholarly editions usually require subsidy. Beyond a modest scale, the difficulty of arranging publication rises disproportionately with length. Of course, an editor must resist cutting size to the point threatening the intellectual integrity or usefulness of the project, but it would be difficult in the present climate of publishing to defend a purist position that all available material should be published, regardless of cost or significance. A degree of self discipline seems called for by the reflection that the greater the subsidy absorbed by one project, the less in a general way will be available for others, perhaps more worthy. Fortunately, in the case of the Marshall correspondence the economic constraint does not seem excessively severe. To reproduce all available material would require an edition of perhaps 1200 pages, while the current plan is for a two-volume edition of some 600–800 pages. There will be some pressure on space, but this is not necessarily bad. There is a natural tendency when considering each item individually to lean in favor of inclusion. This is especially so in the case of items discovered at the cost of considerable effort or ingenuity. When it comes to their own efforts, editors are no less prone than others to lapse into a labor-embodied theory of value. Facing the pressures imposed by the economic constraint can help defend against this bias towards expansion which can result in over-dilution with trivia. In a sense, the second constraint helps the enforcement of the first.

The third constraint faced in the selection process is the copyright one. In recent years copyright questions, especially with regard to manuscript material, have increased in prominence and complexity. The late-nineteenth and early-twentieth centuries are in some ways the most difficult to deal with from a copyright viewpoint – too distant for rights to be closely defined and too close for them to be unenforceable. Permission to publish or republish material from this period seems likely to be forthcoming in all but exceptional cases, and the exercise of gaining permission is to a large extent a *pro forma* one. Nevertheless, when dealing with a large number of collections and correspondents the possibility that copyright considerations will constrain the selection of items needs to be borne in mind. In connection with copyright (as with subsidisation) it is, of course, a great advantage to be operating under the aegis of a major scholarly society, the Royal Economic Society in my case.

These three constraints limit in various ways the selection of material but do not determine it. I have already remarked that the over-riding aim should be to make all *important* primary material available to scholars. But the concepts of "importance" or "significance" are flexible. I do not see how they can be defined meaningfully except with regard to the interests and requirements of a specific audience. Unless everything is to be presented and everything explained, the editor must have in mind, at least implicitly, a conception of the audience to which the work is addressed. For example, there might well be an audience which is especially interested in the forms of dinner invitations or the allocation of lecturing hours in nineteenth-century Cambridge. This is not the audience I have in mind and it will not be well served by my principles of selection. Rather, the audience I envisage is one mainly of economists, especially historians of economics, with a leavening of social scientists from neighboring disciplines, or historians and philosophers of science who may have strayed into the area of economics.[2]

Even granted a general perception of the intended audience, some strategic decisions about coverage are still required. The most important is that of "correspondence" versus "letters". That is, should both "out" and "in" letters, or only "out" letters, be reproduced? In the Marshall case the lack of many "in" letters might seem to tilt the balance towards the "letters" choice, and opting for this would not be a serious impairment. Marshall's letters usually take the form of a

2/ The fact that an edition of correspondence is unlikely to be redone for a generation or more does suggest that it would be unwise to take too narrow and time-bound a view of what kinds of things will be of interest to the audience.

monologue rather than a dialogue. They are occasions to state his own views and attitudes rather than to respond to his correspondent's. His letters could stand alone satisfactorily. Nevertheless, there are enough "in" letters of substantive or illustrative interest to make some inclusion of them desirable, although the criteria for inclusion might well be more stringent than those applied to "out" letters.

Another strategic question concerns letters previously printed, either written by Marshall for the press or published by others since his day. Should the selection from these be handled differently to that from previously unpublished letters? Previous publication lends a certain authority which might suggest comprehensive reproduction of such items. On the other hand, the fact that they are already accessible in print might argue in favor of greater selectivity, especially if space proves tight. Letters already available in full scholarly dress (such as Marshall's correspondences with Walras or Jevons) pose a particular difficulty. To omit them would leave significant gaps in the overall picture, while to include them might require the exclusion of marginal matter of some interest. I expect the former consideration will dominate, but one compromise would be to omit "in" letters in such cases. A particular difficulty arises in the case of previously-published private letters or portions of letters for which the manuscripts can no longer be found. Unfortunately, this is the case for over three quarters of the letters reproduced in *Memorials*. Moreover, a comparison of the texts of the letters published in *Memorials* with the manuscripts which have survived shows that very free editing took place. There are excisions of delicate or tangential matter and rewordings for greater clarity, few of which are indicated in the published versions. Obviously the original manuscripts will be used whenever available, but in other cases it seems better to use the printed versions rather than suppress them. The *Memorials* letters are too widely known and used to be ignored. Many are important, and Pigou's editing, although inappropriate by modern standards, does not seem to render the texts inaccurate in vital ways.

Having settled such strategic issues, the selection of individual letters should not be a difficult matter. The letters divide readily into three groups – definitely in, definitely out, and marginal. (I fear that I am representing everything as coming in triads!) The hope is that the last category will be reasonably small. The kinds of letters likely to be marginal are those which are not themselves of intrinsic interest but have some value in establishing the kind of terms on which the correspondents stood (for example, a formal letter of thanks from the Austrian economist Carl Menger for a copy of one of Marshall's works). Then there are letters which have an incidental interest (for example, an invitation to stay at Balliol Croft which describes the accommodations). Or (and these are the most difficult) there are routine business letters which include a paragraph or a postscript of more general interest. Like the footnotes in the *Principles*, Marshall's postscripts are often of considerable independent interest. Frequently they are added to letters which would not otherwise be worth reproducing. Letters which contain small portions of interest might be handled by partial quotation, perhaps in a footnote. As a general rule, partial quotation seems to me an unsatisfactory compromise. The elisions tantalise the reader and test his faith in the editor's judgement. At the very least, omitted passages ought to be paraphrased briefly. But some recourse to partial quotation might prove necessary to save space and prevent excessive padding with tedious and largely irrelevant matter. Here, as in other cases, the guiding aim should be to make the work as useful as possible to the envisaged audience, given the overall constraints faced.

With selection completed, the final problem is to make it accessible to readers by embodying it in a finished text. It is here that the editor's hand is most obvious, but in some ways least important, for with correspondence the primary material should largely be able to speak for itself no matter how much or little the editor embroiders it. There are many good models for the general layout of an edition of correspondence (the recent Darwin one for example[3]). In Marshall's case there seems no good reason for departing from the usual chronological presentation, with each letter separately annotated and a brief biographical framework provided. Nor are there any noteworthy problems involved in transcribing the original texts for publication. There are the usual problems of a few illegible or ambiguous words, a few apparent lapses of the pen, and a few inadequately dated letters, but none of these pose unusual or important difficulties. It is to the task of footnote annotation that a considerable portion of the editor's efforts must be devoted. The temptation to display one's diligence and erudition should be kept in check, although there is no need to go to Puritan extremes. As in the case of selecting primary material, the choices of what needs to be explained and the degree of detail to which explanation should be taken logically cannot be decided without some conception of the intended audience. It is impossible to explain everything and take nothing for granted. The envisaged audience is likely to have interests and general knowledge not too dissimilar from the editor's own (at least that is the natural bias one is prone to slip into). This means that on important matters editorial explanation and documentation should be straightforward. Because those matters lie well within the range of the editor's sphere of competence, he is likely to know the sources to consult and the explanations needing to be made. He will also be alert to the nuances and allusions which might lead the uninitiated astray. It is a different matter with those tangential matters – obscure names, places, events, etc. – which will be of little interest or importance to the

3/ (Burkhardt & Smith 1985).

audience but about which the editor feels it necessary to report *something*, anything! Such tangential matters are another of the editor's crosses. The amount of effort involved in annotation tends to be inversely proportional to the importance of the point being explained. For when the editor gets to or beyond the fringes of his range of competence he must tackle new and strange areas of knowledge and find his way around unfamiliar information sources. Not only will this take much time and trouble, but the results will often be extremely unreliable. When editors reach the limits of their competence they tend to become incompetent as well as inefficient. It would probably be preferable, and certainly more honest, to confess to ignorance rather than pretend to an omniscience one doesn't have and is likely to be caught out on.

II

In retrospect I realise that editing Marshall's manuscripts was a rather straightforward task. In the first place, it involved working with a single collection, the Marshall papers and books preserved in the Marshall Library. Secondly, it had a clear significance and focus. Marshall began his work in economics in the late 1860s, but published little besides the small *Economics of Industry* of 1879 until the *Principles* appeared in 1890. His long delay in publishing his ideas, allied with the strong claims he made for subjective priority with respect to the important theoretical developments of the early 1870s – commonly referred to as the neoclassical revolution – made the discovery of his early manuscripts a matter of some note. This manuscript material threw considerable light on the early development of his ideas and the controverted questions of priority surrounding it. There seemed little doubt that making the material more readily available to scholars was a worthwhile enterprise. With the support and encouragement of Sir Austin Robinson, the preparation of an edition was sponsored by the Royal Economic Society and appeared in 1975 as *The Early Economic Writings*.[4]

As in the case of letters, Marshall made no systematic attempt to preserve his papers. Indeed, he was quite ruthless in cannibalising manuscript material rather than recopying it whenever it could be adapted to some later purpose. The papers that have survived – a jumbled collection of manuscript fragments, lecture notes, notes on reading, press cuttings, examination questions, student records, etc. – have never been fully catalogued and probably would not justify the labour of a comprehensive catalogue.[5] But mixed in with this miscellany, which would amount in total to some eight to ten feet of standard shelf space, are some manuscript pieces of undoubtedly early date. These must have been preserved partly from sentiment, but also because Marshall felt that they might be of some use to him. Even in the last year of his life he was toying with his earlier occasional pieces and manuscripts in the hope of editing a collection for publication. Upon his death the task devolved upon Pigou, Marshall's literary executor. Pigou included many of the occasional pieces in *Memorials* but included very little manuscript material other than correspondence.

When I first came upon the material in 1966, largely by accident, its existence was practically unknown or forgotten. My interest was sparked by the recognition that an essay on the theory of value of an apparently early date was the one Marshall had referred to in an 1888 letter to Neville Keynes as "part of the first systematic account of my views on value".

4/ The predominant role played by the Royal Economic Society in general and Sir Austin Robinson in particular in supporting editorial work in economics deserves to be emphasised.

5/ A preliminary list was provided by Rita McWilliams Tulberg (then Rita McWilliams) in 1969. This list raises expectations too high since many of the items listed are in fact jumbled assortments of oddments.

Guillebaud (1961, II, 364–5) had reproduced most of the letter but observed that "there appears to be no record amongst Marshall's papers" of the item described. Yet here it indubitably was. The first idea was to reproduce this "Early Essay on Value" only, but the recognition that there were related items suggested that a more comprehensive edition might be justified. This possibility was reinforced by the unearthing of a major portion of the manuscript of a volume on foreign trade which Marshall had written in the mid-1870s but never published.

The preparation of the edition involved two distinct sets of decisions – selection and presentation. Selection was not difficult. A cutoff in 1890, the year the *Principles* appeared, seemed appropriate, partly because the emphasis was on the early development of Marshall's views, and partly because little unpublished material of substantial interest survived from the later period.[6] Anything bearing directly on the development of Marshall's theoretical views prior to 1890 was a clear candidate for inclusion. Material which threw significant light on his social and policy views prior to 1890 also seemed worth including, but here the decisions were less clear cut. For example, I decided to exclude three essays on "psychology" (really more philosophical than psychological) written by Marshall in the late 1860s as too remote from the other material to be included as part of the text and too extensive to form an appendix. I also omitted (a decision I now somewhat regret) Mary Paley's notes on six lectures Marshall gave to women students in 1873 on "Some economic questions directly connected with the welfare of the labourer". Although of little or

6/ Apart from a considerable number of typescript fragments written for *Industry and Trade* but not used there, fragments which are of no more than mild interest in my view, the only substantial item which might have been included was a manuscript preface or statement Marshall wrote in the early 1890s as part of his work with the Royal Commission on Labour.

no theoretical interest, these do have a period charm.[7] On the whole, though, I tended to err if at all on the side of inclusiveness.

The edition was primarily of manuscript material but it seemed appropriate to include a few previously published items. The most important of these were the two pairs of chapters on "The Pure Theory of Foreign Trade" and "The Pure Theory of Domestic Values" privately printed in 1879 at the instigation of Henry Sidgwick. This printing was for the convenience of a Cambridge discussion group, but a few copies percolated outside Cambridge and the chapters became justly famous although very rare. They were eventually reprinted in facsimile by the London School of Economics (Marshall 1930). The "Pure Theory" chapters were originally appendices to the abandoned foreign-trade volume and the printing was not supervised by Marshall nor was any serious editing performed. It seemed appropriate to return these chapters to their original context and provide them with a fuller editorial apparatus. They were closer to a manuscript version (the original manuscript of them being untraceable) than to a published work. Apart from these "Pure Theory" chapters, two very short previously-published items were included because they were inaccessible. But no attempt was made to reproduce all Marshall's pre-1890 publications, especially the 1879 *Economics of Industry*, as this would have involved a considerable increase in scale.

Having selected the items to be included, the task of editing them and introducing them to the reader remained. Much of the manuscript material selected was rough and incomplete in form – often fragments or preliminary working notes or jottings. Even the more polished manuscript pieces were rarely in a form designed for publication. A frequent further

7/ An outline of the lectures is provided by Rita McWilliams Tulberg (1969, 19).

complication was the existence of later emendations of an undetermined date by Marshall who seems to have worked over his early notes in the later years of his life. It would have been virtually impossible to reproduce the manuscripts exactly as they stood, and even if this could have been done the result would have been of little service to the reader by being needlessly complex and distracting. In the case of a social scientist like Marshall, substance is more vital than form. The editorial procedures appropriate for, say, a major poet, would be out of place.

By choosing not to reproduce the material *exactly* as it stands, the editor has automatically elected a degree of editorial discretion. How extensive this should be and what precise form it should take are questions which again can only be settled by considering the needs and tastes of a specific audience. In the case of Marshall's manuscripts I adopted certain working rules. For example, when there were emendations of uncertain date I reproduced the earliest version as having greater stylistic uniformity and authenticity of period unless a later working was emphatically clearer. Substantive variations were recorded. Frequent abbreviations, such as xop for "expenses of production", or = ^{m} for "equilibrium", were written out in full, and punctuation made consistent, without noting each change, but other alterations were noted and explained. The dating of much of the manuscript material posed an additional difficulty. Attributions of date often had to be based on physical appearance and internal evidence. Precise dating was rarely possible, but in most cases dating to within a couple of years was possible with considerable confidence.

Even with the manuscript material presented in a reasonably "reader-friendly" form, its frequently scrappy and fragmentary character called for a fair amount of editorial exegesis and articulation. Given the over-riding interest in the early development of Marshall's economic thought, it seemed desirable to include a general study of the implications of the new material for the interpretation of this development. This was accomplished by adding a lengthy general introduction together with short introductions to each item reproduced. This is a more intrusive editorial role than might normally be appropriate when reproducing manuscript material. But it seemed the best solution given the rather unusual situation.

Looking back after the lapse of more than a decade raises a few regrets. There are one or two additional items that might have been included, one or two included items that might have been excluded, minor changes in organisation that might have been made, greater control over type sizes that might have been exercised, typographic errors that might have been corrected, and so on. Unfortunately, a second edition which would give the chance to make such minor adjustments is rarely an option for this kind of scholarly publication. But fortunately, such blemishes, although they loom large in the author's eye, do not seem to detract seriously from whatever value the edition might have.

III

With the conspicuous exception of the *Principles*, Marshall's published works do not pose serious editorial difficulties. A new edition of the 1879 *Economics of Industry* is needed – there has never been a modern reprint and it is now quite scarce – but this would not pose major editorial problems beyond the by-no-means trivial one of how to assemble copies of all the different printings. Changes were made in successive printings, but because the book was stereotyped they tended to be minor – primarily the updating of factual statements and, in 1881, the addition of an amplifying preface.

Apart from the *Principles*, the available editions of Marshall's other published works seem adequate for present scholarly needs. However, the *Principles* is another matter. I can think of no other work in the economics literature posing such serious editorial difficulties. The reasons for this are easily stated. Marshall revised the book seven times, frequently reorganising it and recasting or rewriting large sections. Moreover both his thought and his expository style are complex and subtle. Every edition is a closely woven whole and the changes between editions cannot be identified easily, often involving subtle changes in general perspective or else implicit rebuttals or retractions provoked by criticisms received.

The task of preparing a variorum edition of the *Principles* was undertaken by Claude Guillebaud whose edition appeared in 1961. The approach he adopted was to reproduce as the first volume the full text of the final, eighth, edition of 1920. Editorial indicators were inserted in this text referring to editorial notes in the second volume. These notes identify the date at which any passage was first introduced by Marshall and indicate any minor variations in the passage as it appeared in the earlier editions. Some passages from earlier editions which were not transferred to the eighth, or which were heavily rewritten, are reproduced as appendices in the second volume, together with various supplementary materials from other sources. Editorial explanations are minimal and no systematic attempt is made to elucidate Marshall's sometimes-obscure allusions or to bring the references up to modern bibliographic standards.

Any regular user of the Guillebaud edition, and that includes all scholars who have worked seriously on Marshall, can testify that it is both indispensable and unsatisfactory. It is indispensable because the changes Marshall made were so extensive and important that no one edition represents his thought fully. The eighth edition is by no means the best or most comprehensive. Guillebaud (1961, II, 18) himself thought that the third edition of 1895 was the acme. However, working with all eight editions is rarely possible, and it would be difficult and time consuming, even if feasible, because of the difficulty of locating all the passages relevant to the particular point of interest. The Guillebaud edition certainly fills an important need in allowing at least preliminary access to the various phases in the book's evolution. It is unsatisfactory in several ways, however. The insufficiency of bibliographic and clarificatory notes is a minor drawback. The lack is obvious to the reader and not irremediable. A more serious drawback is that it is quite impracticable, and usually impossible, to reconstruct the texts of any editions before the eighth. But the most basic problem is that not all changes are recorded. As George Stigler (1962) has demonstrated decisively, there are unnoted changes which, although apparently slight, are of considerable significance for the student of Marshall's thought. Stigler counselled against sole reliance on the Guillebaud edition, but it has nevertheless become the standard reference – a fact which tends to conceal its deficiencies. For few scholars have the fortitude to go back and grapple with the earlier editions after a typically-exhausting struggle with the ambiguities and complexities of Marshall's work. Nothing in Marshall's writing is straightforward or clear cut, nevertheless it remains stimulating and insightful. Otherwise it would hardly be worth worrying about editing it.

There is a further problem which Guillebaud overlooked, and that is the problem of "printings". Marshall appears to have introduced minor variations into the reprintings which occurred between successive editions. For example, Guillebaud's first volume, ostensibly the text of the eighth edition of 1920 must be that of a subsequent reprinting as it includes a reference by Marshall to a 1921 publication.[8] The ease with which Marshall was able to make changes reflects his unusual relationship with Macmillan and Company, the publisher of all his books. The actual printing was undertaken in Cambridge at the Pitt Press and entirely supervised by

8/ Guillebaud 1961, I, 99n. The fact is noted by Stigler (1962, 284n).

Marshall, the publishers giving him more or less blanket authority. Marshall was effectively in control of printing and revision with Macmillan's acting rather as risk-sharing agents, performing little in the way of editorial functions. As stocks ran low Macmillan's called for a reprint or new edition, but left Marshall free to doctor the text as he wished. The decision to launch a new edition rather than reprint seems to have been almost entirely Marshall's. It is not clear that such freedom was entirely beneficial to Marshall. It certainly involved him in spending in incessant rewriting much time and effort that might better have been invested elsewhere.

Given the existence of the Guillebaud edition it is unlikely that a new scholarly edition of the *Principles* will be viable in the foreseeable future. Nevertheless, it is interesting to speculate on what form a new edition might take, for the work is certainly a stringent testing ground for theories of variorum editing. Clearly, the Guillebaud edition falls considerably short of being a full variorum edition which conflates all editions while allowing any one to be reconstructed.

Stigler's (1962) conclusion, when reviewing Guillebaud, was that the attempt to provide full variorum editions of works as complex as the *Principles* should be abandoned. However carefully conceived, the results are likely to be unsatisfactory to scholars by being incomplete, or unmanageably complex, or even both. Stigler proposed instead a scholarly version of a single edition supplemented by studies of the evolution of the author's thought on specific topics. His arguments are persuasive if the only alternative considered is a single variorum edition in the standard mold. But there could be other possibilities. One would be to prepare variorum editions of subgroups of individual editions, reducing for example the eight editions of the *Principles* to two or three variorum editions each covering a group of editions between which changes are not unmanageably complex. In Marshall's case, the very large rearrangements involved in the second and fifth editions would complicate such an enterprise, and it could well be that as many as four variorum editions would be necessary – hardly a sufficient improvement on working with all eight originals as to justify the effort and resources needed to produce such works. A more promising possibility would appear to be the abandonment of the printed page for the electronic one. The general notion would be to store electronically the texts of all eight editions and supplement these texts with two kinds of aid, one structured, the other flexible. The structured aids would essentially represent the editor's work. There would be structured indices with more levels of hierarchy than are practicable in a printed index. These would take the user to specific relevant passages. There would be notes, explanatory, biographical, etc., which could be called up in connection with a specific passage. And there would be inter-edition linkages which would allow specific passages to be traced from edition to edition. One could imagine ingenious use of color or character differences to highlight minor verbal changes from one edition to the next. The flexible aids would be user-guided routines which could, for example, search for particular word patterns, or locate a remembered quotation. Obviously, I am sketching this suggestion in the broadest terms as it seems quite infeasible on economic grounds for such a project to be undertaken in the near future in connection with the literature of economics. Although economists were among the earliest large-scale users of computers, their limited interest in the careful study of the classic texts of the subject will preclude them from being pioneers in the large-scale application of computers to textual matters. Advances here are more likely to occur in the area of the humanities where the large body of interested scholars offers a greater chance of significant payoff to the very large investments of time and effort required. But software developed for one area may prove transferable to others.

IV

I cannot imagine that anything I have said will have significant novelty for those who have been involved in similar enterprises, but it may be helpful to those who have yet to start, although whether as guide or warning I must leave the reader to judge. The business of editing seems to me a thoroughly practical and pragmatic one, calling for good sense and a close attention to detail. There are few significant guiding principles and one mainly learns inductively by following excellent models and tackling the specific problems arising as best may be. The editing of the writings of economists does not appear to involve distinctive problems of a noteworthy sort, but it is addressed to a distinctive audience, one more interested in ideas and substance than in style and literary form. This fact, if anything, is what differentiates editorial work in economics from that in many other areas.

Works Cited

Burkhardt, Frederick and Smith, Sydney (eds.) 1985, *The Correspondence of Charles Darwin*, Cambridge: Cambridge University Press.

Guillebaud, C.W. (ed.) 1961, see Marshall 1961.

Marshall, Alfred 1930, *The Pure Theory of Foreign Trade: The Pure Theory of Domestic Values*. Reprints of Scarce Tracts in Economic and Political Science, No. 1, London: London School of Economics.

— 1961, *Principles of Economics*, 9th ed. (ed. C.W. Guillebaud), London: Macmillan.

McWilliams Tulburg, Rita 1969, "The Papers of Alfred Marshall Deposited in the Marshall Library, Sidgwick Avenue, Cambridge", *History of Economic Thought Newsletter*, 2 (November), 9–19.

Robbins, Lord 1977, Review of Whitaker 1975, *Economica*, N.S., 44 (February), 91–2.

Stigler, George G. 1962, "Marshall's *Principles* after Guillebaud", *Journal of Political Economy*, 70 (November), 282–6.

Sturges, Paul 1975, *Economists' Papers 1750–1950: A Guide to Archive and other Manuscript Sources for the History of British and Irish Economic Thought*, Durham: Duke University Press.

Whitaker, John K. (ed.) 1975, *The Early Economic Writings of Alfred Marshall, 1867–1890*, 2 vols., London: Macmillan.

On Editing Keynes*

D.E. Moggridge

The Collected Writings of John Maynard Keynes[1] taken as an edition is notable for the rather scanty discussion of the editorial principles and problems involved. In each of the published volumes, all the reader receives is a five page general introduction which, except for the changing size of the enterprise and the personnel involved in the edition, is common to all volumes, and a brief editorial note of one, two, or three pages which mentions particular sources and, very occasionally, particular editorial problems.

In this paper, I will amplify this rather sparse discussion

*I should like to thank Sue Howson, David Laidler, Sir Austin Robinson, Aubrey Silberston and Donald Winch for helpful comments on earlier drafts.

1/ Throughout, reference to the edition will take the form JMK, volume number, page numbers. A full list of the volumes appears as Appendix I.

of the editorial principles involved in the over 13,000 pages of text now available in the 29 volumes published between 1971 and 1983. (There is a volume of index and bibliography still to come.) In doing so, I will have to subject you to the results of some historical research, because I only became involved with the edition in 1969, fifteen years after the conception of the enterprise. By that stage, many decisions of principle had already been taken and some volumes were very well advanced.

Maynard Keynes died on 21 April 1946. Inevitably, the Royal Economic Society considered a memorial to the man who had edited the *Economic Journal* between 1911 and 1945, had been Secretary of the Society between 1913 and 1945 and was President of the Society at the time of his death. The discussions began in February 1951. To judge from the minutes of the Council of the Society and the surviving correspondence,[2] a number of possibilities were considered: an annual lecture, the establishment of a reading room for members of the Society in the proposed new premises of the Royal Statistical Society, a travelling fellowship for younger scholars, the publication of original work in economics, a series of fine editions of the great economists, which would extend the Sraffa edition of Ricardo then approaching publication, and an edition of all or part of Keynes's own writings. Most of these ran into problems in the eyes of participants in the discussions: too many existing endowed lectureships, the capital sums involved, difficulties with the Inland Revenue, or the fact that existing market institutions seemed to work

2/ For an indication of the matters raised, see the minutes of the Council of the Royal Economic Society, 22 February 1951, 17 May 1951 and 20 November 1952, as well as E.A.G. Robinson to Lord Brand, 24 September 1952. The minutes of the Council of the Society are on deposit in the British Library of Political and Economic Science, while all the letters referred to are in the possession of Sir Austin Robinson.

reasonably well, thus making subsidies unnecessary. This last objection, what might almost be called the economist's gut reaction when questions of subsidies or institutional change are raised, applied initially even to the publication of Keynes's own writings. As Austin Robinson, who in an obituary of Keynes had advocated the publication of some of Keynes's Second World War state papers (1947, 142), put it to Lord Brand, then President of the Society on 24 September 1952:[3]

> Almost anything of Maynard's that should be published (and we certainly feel that some of the unpublished material ought some day to be published) will have a sufficiently good market for a subsidy to be unnecessary.

In fact, in the early 'fifties there were two proposals for collections of Keynes's writings under consideration outside the Society. Richard Kahn, Keynes's literary executor for his professional writings, was thinking of two volumes of previously published and unpublished materials including, he hoped, some of the wartime memoranda.[4] Seymour Harris, Keynes's leading American publicist, while believing that a complete edition of his previously published writings (which he estimated at 2.3 million words or 20 300-page volumes) was probably uneconomic, had a project for publishing commercially six volumes of Keynes's writings not available in the seven books and two volumes of essays in economics Keynes published in his lifetime. Such a project he suggested would make available 60 per cent of Keynes's published

---

3/ Or as the minutes of the Council of 22 February 1951 say such a proposal was "better regarded as an ordinary publishing proposition than as an appropriate form of commemoration".
4/ R.F. Kahn to S.E. Harris, 9 June 1953; E.A.G. Robinson to Lord Brand, 24 September 1952.

writings not previously available in book form.[5] Such an edition, he estimated, would sell 5000 copies worldwide. The only continuing advocate of a "complete works" with Royal Economic Society support was Roy Harrod, Keynes's official biographer (1951, 467).[6]

In the autumn of 1953, with nothing underway and the prospects of raising large sums of money in the United States not very favourable, the Council of the Society discussed the question of a memorial again. In the end, the proposal for a travelling fellowship was referred back to the committee set up to consider it in November 1952. However, the Committee, to which were added Richard Kahn and Roy Harrod, was also asked "to consider the possibility of commemorating Lord Keynes through a series of fine editions of the great economists thus extending the project for the publication of Ricardo to which Lord Keynes had given great thought" and "to give further consideration to the possibility of a similar edition of Lord Keynes' collected works".[7] The enlarged committee, or, more accurately, those members of it who were in London on the day, met at the Reform Club on 5 January 1954. The main topic under discussion was only one edition, Keynes's collected works. Those taking part, Roy Harrod, Richard Kahn, Humphrey Mynors and Austin Robinson, foresaw difficulties, but thought them surmountable, and recommended to the Council that such an edition proceed. On 13 May 1954, "after a lengthy discussion", the Council agreed:

5/ S.E. Harris to R.F. Kahn, "Further Publication of Lord Keynes' Writings", 19 November 1953.

6/ E.A.G. Robinson to R.F. Kahn, 3 November 1953.

7/ Minutes of the Council of the Royal Economic Society, 29 October 1953, item 7. The original committee had consisted of Lord Brand, Robert Hall, Humphrey Mynors, Lionel Robbins and Austin Robinson.

(a) that the memorial to Lord Keynes should take the form now proposed;
(b) that a start should be made with an edition of Lord Keynes' writings published and unpublished;
(c) that the responsibility should be delegated to Professor Kahn, Mr. Harrod and the Secretary in consultation in all financial matters with the Treasurer for the time being;
(d) that the Committee be authorised to spend in the first year a sum not exceeding £1000, and to employ...on a full-time basis Mrs. E. Johnson to work under the direction of the Committee;
(e) that the Committee be instructed to report progress at intervals to the Council.

The edition and the employment of its first volume editor were thus authorised.

To judge from Austin Robinson's notes from the January Reform Club meeting and his subsequent correspondence with Daniel Macmillan, Keynes's publisher, in June 1954, certain crucial decisions were made at an early stage. First, and perhaps most important, the edition would not encompass all of Keynes's writings. As Austin Robinson's notes put it, "Not like Ricardo" – the Society's ten volume edition under the editorship of Piero Sraffa then being published. The Keynes edition would consist of Keynes's previously published books and uncollected published letters and articles, plus "a limited publication of Keynes' more important correspondence on economic issues, mainly of an academic nature".[8] It was to be "Not like Ricardo" in another sense: it was to be "minimalist" in the case of previously published work, "a reprinting – with a minimum of purely explanatory footnotes", as Austin Robinson's notes put it. Finally, the edition would be printed by Cambridge University Press and

8/ E.A.G. Robinson to D. Macmillan, 14 June 1954.

published by Macmillan "provided that we [Macmillan] do not incur any financial risk – in fact on a commission basis".[9]

At the time these decisions were taken, those involved in the project did not have a complete picture of the raw materials from which they would build the edition. For published works, they had R.J. Spencer Hudson's *Towards a Bibliography of John Maynard Keynes* (1950) with its 806 items, but it was admittedly incomplete. For unpublished materials, they had Keynes's professional papers which would eventually fill six four-drawer filing cabinets and more than three cupboards, but these were unsorted and uncatalogued. Moreover, some of the professional papers were still subject to the Official Secrets Act which at the time had a 50 year rule for access to public records. This embargoed anything in the papers produced by Keynes during his official career and prevented access to the public archives, where, in addition to papers on the day-to-day departmental files, there was Keynes's own private office collection from 1940–6 running to over 125 files. It is true that Roy Harrod had been through the Cambridge Keynes papers and Keynes's private office files when preparing his biography, but writing a biography and estimating the extent of what might, if it were released between 1957 and the end of the century under the existing rules, become part of the edition are rather different exercises.[10] Thus it was inevitable that it would be some time before the exact scope and extent of the edition were clear.

The successful career of Harry Johnson further complicated matters, for when he left Cambridge for a chair in Manchester in 1956 and subsequently proceeded to Chicago

9/ D. Macmillan to E.A.G. Robinson, 22 June 1954; E.A.G. Robinson to D. Macmillan, 23 June 1954.
10/ The rule for opening records in a particular file was 50 years from the year following the date of the last item on the file, unless an embargo of 75 or 100 years existed.

in 1961, Liz lost day-to-day contact with the papers. As a result, progress was slow and from the available records the first statement about the shape and size of the edition did not come until 1961. This statement cast the edition into the quadripartite form that still survives. The first ten volumes would be books published in Keynes's lifetime. There would then follow volumes of academic economic articles and correspondence (two in the 1961 plan) and a volume of social political and literary writings. The plan then envisaged a series of "companion volumes", dealing with Keynes's non-academic contributions to public affairs – letters to the press, speeches, popular articles and selected correspondence. In 1961 the editor and Austin Robinson were thinking in terms of three such volumes, covering 1909–28, 1923–39 and 1939–46. As the overlap indicates, although the volumes were to be broadly chronological, they were to be organised thematically. Finally the edition was to conclude with an index and bibliography. Even at this stage, there were suggestions that 17 volumes might not be enough, but nobody expected the 30 that would eventually appear.

This 1961 decision on the shape of the edition after volume X has caused some discussion, for it differs from the norm for such editions which take materials by type and organise them chronologically within each type with little editorial comment. For example, Sraffa's Ricardo had the classes of pamphlets and papers, speeches and evidence, letters and biographical miscellany and within each class organised everything chronologically. By contrast, the Keynes edition normally mixes document types up and normally attempts to provide in lead-ins to particular documents what is often a running commentary giving the documents a context. As a result, the editor is more intrusive in Keynes than in Ricardo (Patinkin 1975, 250–2).

In some respects I can see the worry, although I think it can be overstated. Over an edition, when that edition is *complete*, it should make no difference in principle how the material is organised. Everything will be there and the reader using a good general index, as he would have to in any case, can get to all the items relevant to the matter at hand. The Keynes edition, however, does not pretend to be complete. In these circumstances, no matter how the edition is organised the reader is inevitably in the hands of the editor's principles of selection, for it is the editorial decision that determines what items from the larger set become available in print. Once this point is accepted, I believe that the question of form is secondary, unless some forms lead to less desirable editorial decisions than others. In the case of the Keynes edition, from the evidence available, I do not believe that the choice of form was made with an ulterior motive. There was certainly no deliberate attempt at hagiography. Moreover, as the original editorial committee of Roy Harrod, Richard Kahn and Austin Robinson did not know the full extent of the material available, was not closely involved in the editorial work and did not, in my experience, interfere in any editorial decisions, it is hard to see what worries one might have in the case of the Keynes edition – unless, of course, the volume editors let the users down. With the full editorial raw material readily available to scholars, there is certainly a check.

As well, I think it can be argued that it is not necessarily a bad thing that the material in the edition should be packaged so that different users with different interests may buy or turn to particular volumes in the first instance. If this means that certain volumes sell better than others, as has been the case with volumes XIII, XIV and XXIX relating to the creation of the *General Theory*, it may prove sensible to increase their availability by producing paperbacks. True, paperback users will still have to go to other volumes of the edition for completeness when they consider a particular issue, but is greater availability a bad thing? The notion that different volumes might have different markets was in the editors' minds from the outset. So too were commercial considerations, which is not surprising given the Society's financial commitment to an edition published on a commission basis.

The number of volumes continued to expand from the 17 of 1961. By 1964 the total was up to 21; by 1969 it was 24; by 1973 it was 25 and it finally stabilised at 30 in 1978, where it remained only by the expedient of having two very large volumes earlier in the sequence – XII with 896 pages and XIX with 923 pages.

The causes of the expansion were various. The most important was the raw material. The shift from a 50 to a 30 year rule for official materials in Britain from 1968 (with the added accelerated opening of all World War II documents from 1972) opened up all the materials relating to Keynes's official and semi-official career in the Treasury and took the number of World War II companion, or, as they were eventually called, activities volumes from one to six as well as playing some role in increasing the number of World War I and inter-war volumes from the original 1½ to six. The departure of Lady Keynes from Tilton, Keynes's country house, in 1975 resulted in the totally unexpected laundry hamper full of papers dealing with the 1930s which arrived in my Cambridge office in 1976. The most visible result of this was volume XXIX, a supplement to the two volumes published in 1973 containing drafts, articles and correspondence relating to the composition and subsequent discussion of *A Treatise on Money* and *The General Theory of Employment, Interest and Money*. New materials, of course, are not only a problem with such modern editions: one only need remember the unexpected discovery in 1943 of the 'Mill-Ricardo papers' at Raheny Co., Dublin, which added a volume of correspondence and a volume of pamphlets and papers to Sraffa's Ricardo, then in page proof. But new material was not the only cause of expansion. The original editorial committee was not itself closely involved in the day-to-day editorial work. That was naturally in the hands of Elizabeth

Johnson and myself. We had some secretarial and administrative assistance, but no substantial editorial assistance. As a result, we only fully realised the extent of a possible volume once we started to assemble the relevant papers. Thus, when I joined the project in 1969, it was expected that one volume, XIII, would do for all the materials relating to the composition of the *Treatise* and the *General Theory*. The actual result in 1973 was two volumes totalling just over 1200 pages, supplemented in 1979 with volume XXIX from the laundry hamper. Such are the risks of small editorial teams.[11]

So much for the scale and basic organisation of the edition. What of the editorial principles involved in the treatment of its contents? Here it is best to take the materials concerned under four headings, subdividing each as necessary. The main headings are: (1) complete books published during Keynes's lifetime (vols. I–VIII); (2) collections of essays published during Keynes's lifetime (vols. IX and X); (3) other material published in Keynes's lifetime; (4) unpublished materials.

With the exception of *Indian Currency and Finance* (1913), Keynes retained remarkable control over his books. He paid the setting, printing, binding and advertising costs, approved all review copies and, after paying Macmillan a commission, kept any remaining profits. This process allowed him to use galleys as we would use photocopies of drafts and circulate them for discussion and reaction. It also meant that he dealt directly with the printers. Given his control over the text, as

---

11/ In the case of the Keynes edition, some reviewers have had more support than the editors. In the spring of 1975, I had a request from Don Patinkin of the Hebrew University of Jerusalem who was then reviewing six volumes of the edition for the *Economic Journal*. (His review article itself grew into a book (Patinkin 1976).) Working himself with three research assistants he asked me if I could get one of my research team to look out some documents for him. He was very surprised to hear that my whole research team (me) was occupied in examining for the Cambridge Tripos.

editors we used as copytext the last corrected text that had passed through his hands, noting the few variants – and those were very few – between first and subsequent printings. (Before 1930, American editions of Keynes's books were set from the British text with no proof corrections by Keynes. After 1930, we should note, the American and English first printings were identical, for, ignoring the U.S. manufacturing condition and thus foregoing copyright protection, Keynes sent sheets directly from R. & R. Clark in Edinburgh to Harcourt Brace for binding.[12] As reprinted, the volumes were diplomatic reprints, with no attempt to keep the pagination tied in to the literature generated by the earlier editions except in the cases of *A Treatise on Money* and the *General Theory*. For the former we provided a concordance, while for the latter we provided a line for line reprint. Except in two cases, *A Tract on Monetary Reform* and the *General Theory*, the only additions to the texts were foreign prefaces. As a substantial proportion of the *Tract* was a reworking of articles published in the *Manchester Guardian Commercial*'s Reconstruction in Europe supplements, rather than reprint the original articles elsewhere in the edition we provided a list of variants from the articles with the text. In the case of the *General Theory*, a volume with a large student demand which appeared in paperback simultaneously with its appearance in hardback in the edition, we added as appendices two articles where Keynes corrected two mistakes in the book.[13]

The only changes we made to Keynes's literary style, which had been set to Macmillan's changing house style, was to reduce capitalisation and regularise such matters as

12/ This has meant that subsequent American reprintings have not incorporated any of the corrections made in Britain. However, the only volume with significant corrections was the *General Theory*.

13/ "Fluctuations in Net Investment in the United States", September 1936, and "Relative Movements of Real Wages and Output", March 1939.

hyphenation. We were guided by Keynes's own practice in his other writings and surviving manuscripts that had not been house-styled, as well as by Mrs. Stephens, his secretary for the last 12 years of his life.[14]

When it came to the two collections of essays published by Keynes during his lifetime, *Essays in Persuasion* (1931) and *Essays in Biography* (1933), we faced other problems. *Essays in Biography* was the simpler. The question was whether we could add to the volume further biographical essays. We had a precedent, for Geoffrey Keynes, to whom the copyright had been left, had published a posthumous edition of the book (1951) with three additional essays, "William Stanley Jevons" (1936), "Mary Paley Marshall" (1944) and "Newton: The Man" (1942). With this precedent, after discussion with Sir Geoffrey, we decided to include all such biographical material in the volume, plus the autobiographical *Two Memoirs* (1949).

Essays in Persuasion presented more of a problem and much more discussion. In its original form the volume was a collection of selections from books, parts of pamphlets and articles written between 1919 and 1931. In two cases, parts of the books were themselves originally articles.[15] We had a number of options. We could reprint the book as it stood, but this would mean that every item would also appear elsewhere (in the original book, in the full reprinting of the pamphlet or in the full reprinting of the article). At the other extreme, we could avoid the problem of repetition by eliminating *Persuasion* as a separate volume. This had the advantage of tidiness, but it would remove a volume that had proved popular and which probably had a larger potential market than most other volumes in the edition. In the end, we chose a middle way: we maintained the volume, but produced full

14/ M.S. Stephens to E.A.G. Robinson, 7 March 1966.
15/ The books were *A Revision of the Treaty* (1922) and *A Tract on Monetary Reform* (1923).

texts of the articles and pamphlets making it clear how Keynes had edited the originals. For the sake of completeness, we then added Keynes's two post-1931 pamphlets *The Means to Prosperity* (1933)[16] and *How to Pay for the War* (1940), thus enhancing the book's reputation as a good introduction to Keynes's ideas.

The final class of previously published materials was composed of articles, letters to the editor, prefaces, evidence to official committees, reviews and the like. For copytext we used the original British text over which we knew Keynes had control, except in the case of the few American articles never published in England, leaving the mention of syndication to the bibliography. Our only exceptions to our copytext rule came with articles in the popular press, where editors had a penchant for breaking up Keynes's paragraphs and adding sub-headings. In these cases where we had a manuscript, we restored Keynes's paragraphing and removed the sub-headings.[17] We have not in the edition made a note of foreign variants, although we know that Keynes was widely syndicated and that in Nazi Germany, for example, articles such as "National Self-Sufficiency" were altered substantially without Keynes's consent.[18]

16/ *The Means to Prosperity* produced further problems, because the American version differed substantially from that produced for an English audience, for in addition to adding some local references, Keynes had added to the text a re-working of a subsequent popular article, "The Multiplier". In this case, we used the American version as copytext and noted the variants from the original.

17/ In one case, a BBC Broadcast of 1936 "On Reading Books" where an edited version appeared in *The Listener*, we printed the version actually broadcast indicating the editorial changes (JMK, XXVIII, 329–35).

18/ The major changes in that article (JMK, XXI, 233–46) all occurred in Section V (pages 242–6), where he turned to discuss contemporary movements towards national self-sufficiency and economic nationalism. There the translator and editors removed over 50 lines of text and made several

Thus far, I have been dealing with signed, published materials. However there were unsigned and pseudonymous published pieces to consider. With one exception (JMK, XVI, 157–61) these came from three sources: the *Economic Journal*, which had a practice of publishing short, unsigned notes of books to which it did not give regular review treatment; the *Nation and Athenaeum*, of which Keynes was chairman from 1923, and on occasion acted as editor when Hubert Henderson was on holiday, and where he was closely involved in the paper's affairs;[19] and the *New Statesman and Nation* of which he was chairman from 1931 to 1946. In the edition, we only attributed unsigned material to Keynes if we had proof it was by Keynes. This proof could take a number of forms. In the one case of an unsigned *Economic Journal* book note it was a handwritten letter to his Assistant Editor, Austin Robinson, enclosing the note (JMK, XXIX, 273–5). Similar evidence was available for several reviews Keynes inserted in the *New Statesman* (JMK, XXVIII, 8–10, 21–2, 128–30). An alternative source of evidence was marked copies of the *Nation*, although the set in the Keynes Papers was incomplete and the complete set was a victim of the Blitz. Finally, there was a scrapbook of unsigned and pseudonymous pieces from the *Nation* which overlapped in parts with the marked set and which was opened by Keynes's mother on his instructions.[20]

false translations. I am indebted to Professor Knut Borchardt of the University of Munich for this information.

19/ One early bibliography of Keynes's writings (Harris 1947, 670–86) included 112 anonymous articles from the *Nation* using as its criterion of selection articles which "seem to have been written by him or greatly influenced by him". In reaction, Roy Harrod (1951, 327) asserted that "Keynes contributed nothing to the paper which was not signed or initialled, save for one note on Bonar Law".

20/ "I should like very much to have a new volume of my *Nation* articles. But I shall have to mark a copy for you, since I write more than I sign." (Keynes Papers, JMK to F.A. Keynes, 24 June 1923.)

In these circumstances, we cannot claim to have caught all printed unsigned or pseudonymous material from Keynes's pen, but we can claim certainty as to the authorship of what we have published. Others might be less cautious.

I turn now to the last broad class of materials in the edition, those previously unpublished.[21] In two cases in this class, his evidence to the Chamberlain-Bradbury Committee on the Currency and Bank of England Note Issues (1924) and his eight sittings of 'private' evidence to the Macmillan Committee on Finance and Industry (1930) of which he was a member, we had no problem. We treated it the same way as the published evidence. Otherwise, we had inevitable problems of selection. Keynes, perhaps because he did not move College rooms after 1910 or house after 1916, kept almost everything. So too, with some exceptions, do modern bureaucracies. Thus even if we stuck to our initial rule of thumb and did not publish personal correspondence, except for the occasional extract from a letter to his parents or to Lydia to set the stage for a document, thus excluding a large volume of material,[22] we still had problems of selection – unless we were thinking in terms of an edition of 75 or more volumes, some of which would consist solely of such exciting materials as rejection letters for submissions to the *Economic Journal*, letters to his stockbroker or the Inland Revenue, or annotations on the letters, minutes or papers of other civil servants. In dealing with the selection procedures followed by the editors with this material, I shall take several distinct types.

In two cases, we aimed at publishing the complete substantive surviving correspondence on both sides. The first was the

21/ Except, perhaps in part, in Roy Harrod's biography.
22/ Between 1922 and 1937, every day they were apart Lydia and Maynard exchanged letters. As Keynes was normally in Cambridge for three days a week for over 20 weeks each year, the volume of this correspondence alone is considerable – and fascinating.

Keynes-Kingsley Martin correspondence concerning the *New Statesman* and its editorial policy which, with related Keynes articles and letters, covers the first 222 pages of volume XXVIII. The second related to the discussions of drafts and post-publication discussion of the *Treatise on Money* and the *General Theory*. Here it was demanded by D.H. Robertson and agreed with the other major participants – R.F. Harrod, R.G. Hawtrey, R.F. Kahn, and Joan Robinson (all of whom, except Robertson, survived to read their own proofs) – that we would print both sides of the correspondence in full. In these cases, the participants (or in Robertson's and Martin's cases, their executors) ensured that our collection of letters was complete and that our carbons of Keynes's letters reflected everything in the original as actually dispatched. With other discussants of particular aspects of both books we attempted to follow the same principle, although we did have more trouble getting originals. The results appear in volumes XIII, XIV and XXIX.

Otherwise we were selective. In some cases, such as Keynes as editor of the *Economic Journal* or as a referee, we took examples as in volume XII.[23] In others, such as the 1929 controversy with Bertil Ohlin over reparations, the reprinting of Keynes's articles required the correspondence, for Keynes's rejoinder to Ohlin's reply began:

> I have found difficulty in making sure that I understood Professor Ohlin's argument in his article printed above. I have, however, had the benefit of some correspondence with him. (JMK, XI, 468)

The result was the publication of all or parts of 11 letters

23/ There are other examples in volumes XIII, XIV and XXIX, for inevitably discussion of Keynes's two great theoretical books spilled over into the *Economic Journal*.

between the two. There are similar cases from the period of the *Treatise* and *General Theory*. In the Activities volumes, leaving aside for the moment the two world wars when Keynes was either an official (1915–19) or a 'demi-semi-official' (1940–6) (JMK, XXVI, 400), our approach was to use unpublished correspondence, memoranda, speeches, etc. as illustrations of how Keynes supplemented his public attempts at persuasion with other means. One outstanding example is the campaign surrounding the war financing proposals of *How to Pay for the War* (JMK, XXII, ch. 1), where his letters and memoranda not only show him acting to orchestrate his activities with those of others but also provide a running commentary on his activities behind the scenes. In other words, in these cases the main purpose of the selected correspondence is to supplement the published record to show the extent of Keynes's activities.[24]

With the two world wars and Keynes's service in the Treasury, of course, much much less was published and we were forced into the public archives as well as Keynes's own papers not to fill out a published record but to get at the record itself. In what follows I will confine myself to examples from 1940 to 1946, if only because of my experience in producing the relevant six volumes of the *Collected Writings* (XXII–XXVII). The raw materials for the period were vast, not only in volume but also in scope.[25] Throughout the period after

24/ At this point it is probably worth emphasising another point that some seem to have missed. The volumes are the *Collected Writings of John Maynard Keynes*, not of anyone else. It should not be surprising if we do not print every scrap of correspondence between Keynes and some other economist, especially as much of it may tell us little or nothing about Keynes although quite a bit about the other economist. For misapprehensions as to our completeness, see Presley 1978, Part II, ch. 2.

25/ When I was researching the volumes, I emerged from the Treasury papers with some seven feet of photocopies plus two filing drawers of 5″ x 8″ cards containing notes.

August 1940 Keynes had a room in the Treasury, something to which he was not entitled by his official position as a member of one advisory committee. Once there he installed his own secretary, Mrs. Stephens, and proceeded. From that room, he regarded not the Treasury but the whole of Whitehall as his parish. His sources of information varied: his door was open to everyone in his Department; his reading of official papers was voracious, if selective; his network of friends and colleagues inside and outside of Whitehall was well developed. Thus Keynes could, and did, turn up in the oddest places to discuss the oddest issues. Some of his forays were ephemeral, some misconceived, some of long-lasting importance. Most left a trail of letters, minutes, memoranda, annotations or comments on the papers of others and the like. How did we select?

Some topics were self-selecting. It was obvious that wartime budgetary policy, employment policy, the proposals for an international clearing union, the origins of the International Monetary Fund, lend lease, and the events leading up to the 1945 Anglo-American Loan Agreement would be on everyone's list. But even within those, we had to be selective, given the space available. Nor would one want us to print everything, if only because there was considerable repetition, as, for example, in the letters written to journalists and many economists in reply to their comments on the clearing union proposals when they appeared as a White Paper in 1943. In each of these cases, what I tried to do was to provide a documentary history of Keynes's involvement in the issue, even its technicalities, and the evolution of his views. In each case, one published Keynes's major memoranda and supplemented them with letters, minutes, telegrams, records of meetings or marginal comments, publishing both sides of an exchange where it was necessary to understand fully the matters at issue. The record as published is not complete, but I hope I have been as accurate as possible in delimiting

Keynes's role and, in cases of dispute, the exact issues at stake. Thus far, I have discussed the "obvious" wartime activities and interventions. With minor activities different considerations applied. Given that it was necessary to introduce documents to give readers some context and to take them onwards from the document to results, if any, as a matter of general principle I did not include documents which had no result unless they contributed to a later state of opinion which showed up elsewhere in the volume. This ruled out many of Keynes's misguided flurries. I also tended to rule out documents which might have had results and which certainly showed Keynes's mastery of detail but where explaining the details might require vast amounts of editorial explanation. I am thinking here of Keynes's role in shaping the details of many post-war exchange and payments agreements. In other words, I tried to take minor examples which were typical of the whole without bogging the user down in minor details, for even with the edition the serious historian of a particular policy will have to use the archives in the end.

The final type of unpublished document I should discuss are drafts. Here the major problem was the *General Theory*, but there are also examples from 1940–6, most notably the clearing union, and some of Keynes's replies to criticisms of the *Treatise on Money* and the *General Theory*. In the case of the *General Theory*, all the pre-publication correspondence with Harrod, Hawtrey, Kahn, Robertson and Joan Robinson, concerned page and galley proofs, most of which survived along with several earlier drafts. In the other cases, there was also extensive correspondence and recorded discussion of earlier drafts before the documents in question were published or became the subject of international negotiation. With the *General Theory* the decision was to publish every draft, a task made easier by the fact that in many cases from the penultimate manuscript draft through three sets of proofs it was possible to do a collation of variants, keyed line by line into the finally published text which allowed the reader to reconstruct the points under discussion in the correspondence. The result takes up pages 351 to 512 of volume XIV. With this experience behind us, handling the other cases was child's play. In the remaining cases of drafts discussed in the correspondence or surviving in the papers, either the drafts did not survive, as in the case of *A Treatise on Money*, or they were not discussed, so we saw no need to print them.

There is one case, however, where extensive drafts and related unpublished papers do exist where we did not do a serious editorial job. Here I am referring to *A Treatise on Probability* (1921). As subsequent recent work has pointed out (O'Donnell 1982, Skidelsky 1983; Lawson and Pesaran 1985; and Carabelli 1986) there is a substantial body of unpublished material – two fellowship dissertations, further drafts and proofs, correspondence and early papers for the Cambridge Apostles – related to the creation of the *Treatise* and this material, plus the published book, has some relevance to Keynes's work as an economist. It is the case that the editors knew of the materials, but, along with the rest of the profession at the time the relevant decisions were made, regarded *Probability* and the related publications as *sui generis* and belonging more to technical philosophy than economics. As a reflection of this, they asked a philosopher to provide an introduction to *Probability* which would make the enterprise intelligible to non-philosophers, something they did for no other volume in the edition, and merely reprinted the book as volume VIII – out of chronological order – and put the articles in one of the "academic" volumes. As a result, even with the Keynes edition, there is scope for another editorial project.

In discussing the *Collected Writings*, I have emphasised our problems of selection and general treatment rather than those of emendation or the supporting apparatus, largely

because of the way the edition has turned out.[26] Central to
that process was the early dictum of Austin Robinson, who
has nurtured the edition since its beginnings back in the 1950s
and still continues to provide guidance and protection from
the Treasurer of the Royal Economic Society. It was "Not
like Ricardo". This plus the volume editors' historical training
have done much to shape the final product. Perhaps we carried
minimalism too far: there was certainly a reaction on the part
of this editor towards providing the reader with more information about persons, events and the like. Perhaps we should
have been less good examples of what Fredson Bowers has
called "the British dilettante school" (1981, 63). If we had
done so, it would have slowed the edition down, unless we
had further support. And this is important, for, except for
some support from the Canada Council and SSHRCC, the
whole edition, including publication costs, has been borne by
the Royal Economic Society. Yet since 1973 it has been self-
sustaining, only publishing new volumes as the proceeds from
old have warranted it, and more recently having repaid the
Society for its stocks and work in progress, it has started to
make a substantial net contribution to the coffers of the Society. One hopes that the Society, even if the experience of
Keynes and Ricardo have scared it off further large-scale multi-
volume works published on a commission basis, will use some
of Keynes's net proceeds to fulfil the rest of the Council's
minute of 13 May 1954 and continue the "series of fine editions
of the great economists" as it has done in part with Jevons,
Marshall and the Economic Advisory Council.

26/ I have also not mentioned the way we dealt with Keynes's financial
activities for himself, his College and several firms. Here we, with the aid
of Keynes's papers and the co-operation of the College, were able to reconstruct his activities and illustrate them and the attitudes involved with correspondence. The results appear as chapter 1 of volume XII.

Appendix I

The Collected Writings of John Maynard Keynes

Published for the Royal Economic Society by Cambridge University Press
(United States and Canada) and Macmillan.

Works Cited

Carabelli, A. 1986, *On Keynes's Method*, Cambridge University Ph.D. Dissertation.

Harris, S.E. 1947, *The New Economics: Keynes' Influence on Theory and Public Policy*, London: Dobson.

Harrod, R.F. 1951, *The Life of John Maynard Keynes*, London: Macmillan.

Hudson, R.S. 1950, *Towards a Bibliography of John Maynard Keynes*, King's College, Cambridge.

Keynes, J.M. 1971– , *The Collected Writings of John Maynard Keynes*, (eds. E. Johnson and D. Moggridge), 30 vols., London: Macmillan.

Lawson, T. and Pesaran, H. (eds.) 1985, *Keynes' Economics: Methodological Issues*, Armonk, N.Y.: M.E. Sharpe.

O'Donnell, R.M. 1982, *Keynes: Philosophy and Economics – An Approach to Rationality and Uncertainty*, Cambridge University Ph.D. Dissertation.

Patinkin, D. 1975, "John Maynard Keynes: From the Tract to the General Theory", *Economic Journal*, LXXXV (March), 249–71.

Patinkin, D. 1976, "Keynes' Monetary Thought: A Study of its Development", *History of Political Economy*, VIII (Spring), 1–150.

Presley, J.R. 1978, *Robertsonian Economics*, London: Macmillan.

Robinson, E.A.G. 1947, "John Maynard Keynes 1883–1946", *Economic Journal*, LVII (March), 1–68, reprinted in Wood (1983), vol. 1.

Skidelsky, R. 1983, *John Maynard Keynes: Hopes Betrayed 1883–1920*, London: Macmillan.

Wood, J.C. (ed.) 1983, *John Maynard Keynes: Critical Assessments*, 4 vols., London: Croom Helm.

Keynes's Lectures, 1932–35: Notes of a Representative Student. Problems in Construction of a Synthesis*

T.K. Rymes

The Setting

In the early 1930s the United Kingdom suffered a worsening of the economic conditions it had experienced in the 1920s. The poor economic conditions of the earlier decade, rather than improving, showed not only a stubborn recalcitrance but also a discouraging tendency to deteriorate. The economic thinking of the day encompassed swings in economic activity so that while boom might be followed by bust, downturns

*I thank for their comments at the Conference, David Laidler, Scott Gordon and Tom Asimakopulos. In particular I record my indebtedness to Donald Moggridge for his relentless criticism of my work and constant encouragement and support. I acknowledge as well with much appreciation written comments on an earlier version from Don Patinkin. Throughout references to *The Collected Writings of John Maynard Keynes* will take the form JMK, volume number, page number.

would be followed by recoveries. (See, for example, Robertson 1926, von Hayek 1931, and V.C. Smith 1936.) Long lasting and deepening slumps in economic activity for whole economies were, by and large, save for the Marxian analyses of crises, either ruled out by the argument that economies would automatically dig themselves out of the economic pits or would be prevented from recovery by all kinds of restrictions on prices and quantities imposed by special interest groups such as trade unions with market power or through Governments which, however well-intended, impeded recovery and conceivably could worsen slumps. The idea that market economies, depressed below full utilization of available factors of production, might *not* eventually claw their way back to the full employment of labour, land and capital was a nightmare of general economic glut, contemplated but not explained by only a handful of what were considered, if not lunatic, certainly an *outré* group of cranks.

The slump in the U.K., with similar conditions elsewhere in Europe, America, Canada and Australia, was a disease that seemed to afflict most modern capitalist enterprise economies. Certainly from the U.K. vantage point, at least, something was clearly and dramatically wrong.

The Victorian promise of unimpeded progress in scientific achievement, economic accumulation, profitability and high and rising levels of real wage rates and incomes and consumption and social and artistic amelioration and advancement, already staggering under the hideous blow of World War I, seemed a cruel joke. The world seemed also to be afflicted by growing totalitarian nightmares in Germany, Italy and Russia.

It is the exact truth that the only hope of any of us could see of containing, and eventually maybe reversing, these rising tides of horror seemed to be in the discovery, in time, of some new treatment for the multiplying diseases of a dying capitalism in the shortening list of countries still civilized. And that meant economics, and, since there was nothing serious going on elsewhere in England at the time, economics in Cambridge. (Bensusan-Butt 1980, 28)

Onto a world where economic policy seemed to be of austerity, of sound money and finance, of waiting for the recovery which must logically return, onto this world then burst John Maynard Keynes and the *General Theory*.

To many of the young the reaction was apparently rapture. To quote again Bensusan-Butt (35), who compiled the index for the *General Theory*,

> The mystery of contemporary iniquity had been unveiled by a masterpiece of sustained intellectual effort. All the other tangled turgid stuff which lesser men were producing to rationalise the mess around us simply faded away. Now we all knew why.

Tarshis writes that "...we sensed that at last an economist was coming to grips with the most devastating economic disaster in centuries" (Tarshis 1977a, 51).

Less eulogistically, from an Oxford viewpoint, A.J. Brown states that

> ...an empirically quantifiable multiplier, systematic and quantifiable cycle theories, a theory of the short-term equilibrium level of activity, and the first steps towards dynamising it – all arrived in the 1930s. Keynes was responsible for only a part of them, though a bigger part, probably, than anyone else, and to some of them he was less than welcoming. But to those who were young, and learning, when these things happened, they

blended together into a heady mixture, which seemed
to hold the promise of a new and better economic world.
(Brown 1987)

All of this is high drama,[1] indeed some would claim melo-
drama. The late Harry Johnson asserted that the U.K. state
of affairs was a product of the artificial appreciation of the
pound (Moggridge 1972) and that had policy, based on already
reasonably understood monetary theory of the day, been followed both in the U.K. and the U.S.A. (Friedman & Schwartz
1963, esp. ch. 7), the slump of the Great Depression would
not have occurred and the parochial originality of the *General
Theory* would have been unnecessary (E. & H. Johnson 1978,
76). Yet there surely was a problem and something original
about the *General Theory*. In his last address to the Canadian
Economics Association, Professor Johnson argued in 1976
that Keynes's monetary theory

...involved a process of looking past the models and
problems of pure theory to the real world to which
theory claimed to be a scientific guide, recognizing a
glaring gap between the assumptions and hypothetical
economy of the models and the actual behaviour of the
real world... (Johnson 1976: 1978, 248)

Careful reexamination of the historical record of economic
development and policy in the U.K. in the 1930s would seem
to reveal that there was something wrong with the economy,
the existing theoretical understanding and the policy steps
being pursued to combat the unemployment of the time. (For
different views see Richardson 1961 and Middleton 1985.)
New thinking was required – and there is no doubt that the

1/ A recent account of the intensity of the debate in the early 1930s is
found in Durbin (1985).

new thinking was supplied by Keynes. The *General Theory* was born out of the *Treatise*, debates about it with Robertson, Hawtrey, von Hayek and the members of the "Circus",[2] the state of the economy and the tumult of ideas which surged in Cambridge in the early 1930s (Shackle 1967).

The Objective of the Synthesis of the Lecture Notes

A huge literature exists about Keynes's theory, its originality, its philosophical underpinnings – indeed this literature continues to grow apace as newer and deeper understandings of the problems Keynes was addressing, such as the formation of expectations in a world of incompletable knowledge (Lawson and Pesaran 1985), come to the fore. As well, debate continues to take place at the empirical level, in terms of both what in fact the record of the 1930s was and how successful Keynesian policies, if in fact put into place, would have been.

One insight into what Keynes was after in the early 1930s can be captured by reporting what his students recorded him as saying in his lectures at Cambridge. There are, of course, recollections of Keynes as a teacher (Plumptre 1947 and 1975; Bryce, Salant and Tarshis 1977). The synthesis of such records contains something perhaps more solid. The book is a reconstruction of the notes which some of Keynes's students took at his lectures from 1932 to 1935.

In the central section[3] of the book I report without comment and interpretation what the lecture notes say.[4] In the

2/ The "Circus", its members and its contribution to the writing of the General Theory are discussed in JMK, XII, 337–43 and Kahn (1984).

3/ Two introductory chapters precede the reconstructions. The first chapter draws on this paper, while the second reflects on the known interpretation, by three members of the "Circus", of Keynes's Easter Term 1932 lectures.

4/ In that respect I am indebted to advice from Donald Moggridge and Sir Desmond Lee of Wolfson College, Cambridge. The latter, in particular, synthesis, I have eliminated errors in spelling, filled in *obvious* blanks, elaborated *obvious* shorthands, corrected notation, incorrect dates and so forth and supplied the necessary references.[5] At this point, however, I set out some major difficulties confronting the editing of the lecture notes. I then turn to a discussion of the detailed problems of collecting and transcribing the notes.

Major Problems Confronting the Synthesis of the Lecture Notes

The major problem involved in constructing a synthetic version of the lecture notes follows from the remarks quoted already from some of Keynes's students. There can be no doubt that his students were captured, not necessarily completely captured, but captured nonetheless by the belief that Keynes was, in his lectures and in his contemporaneous writings, delving into the very heart of the gravest economic problem of the day. As the lectures progressed, Keynes seemed to them to be shedding theoretical light on a dark and disturbing economic nightmare. Not only that, but as his frequent forays into the public arena attested, Keynes passionately believed that his way of looking at things, his particular shafts

advised me strongly to reflect what students reported together with possible references, and no more! The main part of the volume, in which I have not engaged in explicit interpretation, is thus similar to Lee (1976).

5/ I have constructed as my raw material a companion document, *Keynes's Lectures, 1932–35: Notes of Students*, a reproduction of which is available in the Royal Economic Society in the Marshall Library, Cambridge, in the Keynes Papers in the Library of King's College, Cambridge, and in the MacOdrum Library, Carleton University, Ottawa. That document is the edited and transcribed lecture notes on which my synthesis is based. It is also obtainable, at reproduction cost, from the Department of Economics, Carleton University, Ottawa, K1S 5B6.

of illumination, offered a rationale for policy stances which might conceivably rid the capitalist economies of the evils of lasting unemployment. Here was a heady mixture: a new theory of the economic system as a whole which, while it principally offered an explanation of the existence of widespread and long lasting unemployment, at the same time held out hope for the resolution of much social misery. Small wonder then that Keynes and the *General Theory* were greeted by the young with such enthusiasm.

The apparent rapture of students was with the finished product, that is, with the *General Theory* as it finally emerged in the lectures preceding its publication and with the book itself. Keynes's early lectures may not, it seems, have met with such enthusiasm. Both Bryce and Tarshis, two of the students whose notes form the major part of the synthesis, were so disenchanted after their first year, 1932–33, of economics at Cambridge that they wished to discontinue such studies.[6]

Therein, of course, lies the first and most formidable difficulty involved in the synthesis of these notes and more significantly, in any interpretation of such a synthesis. The difficulty is: How critical are the notes? How aware were the notetakers of alternative viewpoints in economics? The general question to be asked can be illustrated by focussing on two points.

The *General Theory*, Keynes himself states, represented a break with the traditional quantity theory of money[7] and,

6/ At the 1986 Glendon College Conference on Keynes and Public Policy after 50 years, Bryce stated that after a year's study at Cambridge he wrote his parents indicating a desire to switch to physics while Tarshis stated that he was also seeking leave to transfer his fellowship away from economics, a statement he later confirmed in correspondence (Tarshis to Rymes, October 1986).

7/ See, for instance, JMK, XIV, 101–8.

in particular, in the presence of uncertainty, with what the traditional determinants of the rate of interest were deemed to be and how classical quantity of money and the determination of relative values were to be revised into a general formulation[8] of a money theory of value.

Was it recognized that Keynes was trying to construct, not only in the *General Theory* but throughout his theoretical work, a general monetary theory of value? How many of Keynes's contemporaries, colleagues and students conceived of his work along such lines? Certainly the Walrasian tradition had little influence on Keynes. The Austrian tradition at the London School of Economics focussed upon the subjective theory of value, starting principally from exchange economies, and advanced the view that economic systems, because of the relentless search for the gains stemming from increased economic coordination, would be inherently stable with instability, i.e., the problems of the business cycle, stemming largely from unwarranted interference on the part of the monetary authorities. Writing in the von Hayek line of thought, V.C. Smith says that, although the lender of last resort function may still be a necessary central banking function,

> The most satisfactory theory yet offered in explanation of booms and depressions...is one which finds the perpetually disequilibrating force in monetary disturbances expressing themselves in a divergence between the "natural" and market rates of interest and between voluntary savings and real investment (Smith 1936, 4)

and that, after pointing out the many ways in which central

8/ JMK, XIV, 109–23. Townshend (1937) pursued this line of thought with Keynes's encouragement. The correspondence between Keynes and Townshend is in JMK, XXIX, 236–47, 255–9, 288–94.

banks bring about such disruptions, concludes that

> How to discover a banking system which will not be
> the cause of catastrophic disturbance which is least
> likely itself to introduce oscillations and most likely to
> make the correct adjustment to counteract changes from
> the side of the public, is the most acute unsettled
> economic problem of our day. (*Ibid.*, 171)

At Cambridge the "Circus" was concerned apparently with
the attempt to persuade Keynes that the *Treatise* took the
level of output as given at full employment and that a more
general treatment would focus upon and be primarily concerned with the determination of the level of output and
employment. Questions such as the determination of the
relative values of consumption goods and, even more, importantly, of the relative prices of new capital goods and the
absolute money prices of new capital goods were filed into
the background by assuming similar supply conditions in all
activities so that an aggregate real value of output (in wage
units) could be more easily theoretically constructed. While
two of Keynes's closest junior colleagues, Joan Robinson and
Richard Kahn, were working on the determination of relative
values in the short period (Kahn 1929 and Robinson 1933a
and b) in the imperfectly competitive setting, it was not until
the work of Michael Kalecki was more fully recognized that
the integration of the imperfect competition theory of value
and the theory of effective demand was attempted. Even so,
there was still no recognition that Keynes was working on a
monetary theory of value.[9]

The idea that Keynes might be constructing not a general

9/ See Kregel (1985). Keynes's theory became the monetary theory of
output and employment as distinct from a monetary theory of value. For
another illustration of how this point was missed see Eshag (1963).

theory of output but truly a general monetary theory of value was not widely held. Yet it is clear from the *General Theory* that that was Keynes's major theoretical concern. He says

> A monetary economy, we shall find, is essentially one in which changing views about the future are capable of influencing the quantity of employment and not merely its direction. But our method of analysing the economic behaviour of the present under the influence of changing ideas about the future is one which depends on the interaction of supply and demand, and is *in this way linked up with our fundamental theory of value. We are thus led to a more general theory, which includes the classical theory with which we are familiar as a special case.* (JMK, VII, xxii–iii, italics added)

As is so often the case with students, this central theoretical concern of Keynes may not be what drew them to his lecture. The immediate contemporary problem was widespread unemployment. If that were thought to be Keynes's main concern, then Keynes's economics could be considered primarily as depression economics. More comprehensively, the theory of effective demand, i.e. the idea that there exists a theory of total output more general than that determined by the full efficient use of the available factors of production, leads to the belief that only if there is less than full employment does Keynesian economics apply. Once full employment is attained, the classical theory reattains its significance. If this is a plausible view of Keynesian economics, and there is some evidence that, at least on the second point about the special importance of classical economics, Keynes could himself be said to have held such a view (JMK, XXVII, 444), then it follows that Keynesian economics can be expressed primarily in terms of real quantities; consumption, capital formation, and employment. At a time when such real values were languishing Keynes seemed dramatically relevant. Did it really matter that there were other parts of economics which explained the relative prices of consumption goods or which sought to explain the determinant of the aggregate price level? Did it signify to explain the relative commodity structure of consumption when the total volume of consumption was shown to be resting at a low equilibrium level and when it was also shown that the total volume of consumption could be so much higher?[10]

One approaches the lecture notes then with one overriding presupposition, *viz*, the students were not fully aware that Keynes was fundamentally rewriting the theory of value. Rather the students were perhaps primarily concerned with Keynes's work on the "real" events of the day. The focus then was on employment and output!

We can see that if we turn to the notes. The main thread of the notes is supplied by those taken by Lorie Tarshis which span the four years 1932–36. Tarshis was a student of economics before he came to Cambridge. Indeed he recounts that when he arrived at Cambridge in the Fall of 1932 he "...must have been the *Treatise's* most devout believer" (Tarshis 1977, 49). Tarshis defends Keynes's aggregate supply function in terms of the Kahn-Robinson argument that marginal revenue equals marginal cost.[11] Tarshis argues, of course,

10/ Don Patinkin is one who has concentrated upon Keynes's theory of effective demand and stressed its connection with the measurement of "real" national accounting variables. See Patinkin (1976, esp. chs. 10 and 11; 1982; esp. chs. 5 and 9).

11/ See also Tarshis (1978). *Inter alia* Tarshis refers to his notes of Kahn's Michaelmas Term 1932 lectures "The Short Period" for evidence that Keynes's aggregate supply function must be based on the Kahn-Robinson equilibrium level of output for the imperfectly competitive form. An examination of these notes, a copy of which Tarshis made available, certainly reveals the well-known $P = MC(e/e-1)$ formula, where e is the price coming at the *General Theory* through the *Treatise*, that Keynes was attempting to integrate monetary and value theory. He states:

> Monetary theory provided many of the elements for his [Keynes's] analysis of aggregate demand; "value theory" provided the elements for his analysis of the supply counterpart. The aggregate supply function (ASF) was the embodiment or manifestation of the bridge that linked up these two branches of economics (Tarshis 1979, 363; see also Tarshis 1975, 1282–6).

In the imperfect competition discussion in Cambridge in the 1930s, price in excess of marginal cost implies that relative prices would, in general, be related to the distribution of noncompetitive influences throughout the economy. That distribution must be determined, then, in order to work out relative prices and there is nothing in the theory of aggregate or effective demand which permits a solution of that problem, a problem which plagued even Kalecki's version of Keynesian economics. Moreover, Keynes assumed perfect competition in the sense that he never took on board the Kahn-Robinson imperfectly competitive economics of the short period.

More importantly, Keynes's argument about marginal user cost must be considered. In Keynes, marginal user cost is the present value of the expected flow of quasi rents which is foregone by utilizing the capital stock more intensively in the current period. In Keynes's analysis, marginal user cost is part of the marginal prime costs which determine the individual competitive firm's short period level of output. The immediate implication is that the money rate of interest enters

elasticity of demand, but it is not clear that these notes or Kahn's (1929) fellowship dissertation can be interpreted as providing a foundation for Tarshis's interpretation of Keynes's aggregate supply function.

into the determination of that level of output because the present value of the additional future output foregone by using the capital stock more intensively today cannot be determined independently of that interest rate: aggregate supply, as distinct from aggregate or effective demand, is not independent of the money rate of interest. Since the money rate of interest in Keynes is essentially the liquidity premium on money, then the essence of Keynes's monetary theory of value is that the money rate of interest appears as a determinant of aggregate demand and supply and as a component of the price of every capital and consumption good. Here is the kernel of the Keynes-Townshend monetary theory of value.[12]

12/ Sometimes it is argued that Keynes had a different objective when he wrote about user cost. Joan Robinson said:

> Keynes did not take much interest in "marginal revenue". He set up a system of his own – user cost – to account for the excess of price over prime [labour] cost. I think myself that this was not very successful and that Kalecki's conception of the "degree of monopoly" is a better starting point for an analysis of short period prices for manufacturers.

"The contribution of Keynes to economic theory", a lecture given at Carleton University, delivered March 1974 (the date of the lecture was actually 3 April 1976), 3.

In this connection, it is interesting to note the exchange between Tarshis and Austin Robinson which took place at the University of Western Ontario Conference in 1975. I quote (Patinkin & Leith 1977, 79):

> Tarshis: I'd like to ask Austin Robinson whether Keynes took an active part in the other revolution that was underway at Cambridge in the late 1920s and early 1930s – the one that had to do with the theory of value?

> Robinson: I think a quick answer to that is almost none. He saw

With respect to Tarshis, though in his notes he was very careful to capture as much as he could of what Keynes had to say about user cost, it is not clear from any of Tarshis's writings, even at a later date, that he perceived the importance of the marginal user cost and money rates of interest in the determination of relative values. His writings would suggest that he perceived Keynes's user cost as a device to permit Keynes to shift his microeconomics, using national accounting concepts such as gross output and net value added, to macroeconomics.

The next major set of notes, those of Bryce for 1932–34, are characterized by lack of interest in Keynes's lectures on user cost.[13] Indeed, in Bryce's own summary of the *General Theory* there is no mention at all of user cost. As Bryce states (1935, 132):

The general purpose of the theory is to explain the

the manuscript of Joan's *Imperfect Competition* and told Macmillan that, though it might not a[t] first glance look an exciting book to them, they certainly ought to publish it – a surprising but welcome decision. He may have read it with care; he may not have. He was editor of the *Economic Journal*, of course, and published the 1930 'symposium' on "Increasing Returns and the Representative Firm" – the Robertson, Sraffa, Shove exchanges. He was encouraging, he was interested, but he wasn't a partaker in that particular operation.

13/ When Bryce visited Carleton in the Fall 1979 to "read" his notes to me, I remarked to him, when we were examining his notes on user cost, that his attention seemed to have been faltering. He remarked that he believed Keynes's user cost conception was a red herring. In conversations at Toronto in 1983, Tarshis indicated that he thought the conception important indeed, presumably as a device which permitted Keynes to overcome the previously-discussed national accounting problems. It is interesting that the two chief takers of notes who were good friends and to some extent scrutinized each other's notes had such opposing views about Keynes's user cost conception.

determination of, and thereby changes in, total employment and production, and to trace its relation to the amount of investment (capital formation), the rate of interest and the quantity of money.

A major difficulty then associated with any interpretation of the development of Keynes's monetary theory in general and in particular through the medium of the lecture notes taken by his students is the extent of the realization possessed by his contemporaries and students in the 1930s that Keynes was developing a monetary theory of value. The same difficulty confronts the synthesis of the notes.

Another major difficulty must now be confronted. In the economic thinking of the late 1920s and early 1930s an additional question was being discussed. To what extent is the economic system stable? The question of stability concerns both prices and quantities and is concerned with such queries as to what forces would lead prices and quantities to depart from their equilibrium values and how quickly would the disturbed prices and quantities return to such values.

Much of the literature was of the persuasion that the economic system tended to a full equilibrium but that certainly disturbances such as wars, monetary disturbances such as over-expansions on the part of both private and central banks would cause prices and quantities to depart from equilibrium paths, even in a cyclical way. With respect to prices the basic concern was with inflation and particularly runaway or hyperinflation. With respect to quantities there was concern with the collapse of banking systems, falls in industrial production and employment. While it was recognized that the banking system was particularly vulnerable to instability it was widely believed that appropriate behaviour by central banks would eliminate from the economic system the worst aspects of such private banking aberrations. With respect to fluctuations were self-correcting, though, the analysis was not well worked out.

The consequence of this thinking for the interpretation of Keynes's notes follows from the fact that in the *Treatise* Keynes was largely concerned with the determination of the equilibrium levels of the prices of consumption and capital goods, through the mechanism of the equilibration of investment and savings, in a world in which money and, in particular, banking operations were brought to the forefront of the analysis and in which the determination of the levels of total output and employment was not the main topic of concern. Following the "Circus" deliberations and the Hawtrey-Kahn writings on the multiplier, Keynes, in the lectures scheduled for 1931, which were delayed until the Easter Term 1932, was beginning to shift his whole analysis over to the determination, again through investment and savings, of the levels of output and employment. The problem of the determination of the aggregate price level and therefore the mechanics of money supply creation and, in particular, any discussion of the roles played by the private banking system and central banks in the determination of prices other than interest rates were put into the background of the analysis. As a crude caricature, one could say that in the *Treatise*, Keynes took the level of output as given and worked out the determination of relative and absolute prices while by the time of the *General Theory*, he took the level of money wage rates as given so that the level of prices would be determinate, and worked out the determination of the levels of output and employment.

In the *Treatise*, Keynes also dealt with the conditions under which absolute prices could be unstable in the sense of never ending movements in upward and downward directions. It was the investment-savings mechanism which showed that such instability was unlikely, though expectations could be such that equilibrium price levels would not be achieved. It will be noted that such inflations and deflations have nothing to do with the behaviour of the banking system because it was well understood by Keynes that inflationary developments could be generated either by central banks acting, within the context of their monopoly of note issue, to impose inflationary taxes or by the possibility of unstable expansions of the private banking systems undisciplined by central banks. Short therefore of inflationary or deflationary behaviour of the authorities, in the *Treatise* Keynes believed that expectations could be generated wherein the price level would move up or down in a continuous way. Stability might be achieved by the investment-savings mechanism but not necessarily and instability owing to myopic expectations *as well as* the nature of the operations of private banking systems could not be excluded.

In the Easter Term 1932 lectures, Keynes was mainly concerned with the *multiplier analysis* for the determination of the stability of prices. The multiplier was an instrument of analysis which Keynes did not have at his disposal for the *Treatise*. Its absence led to the banana plantation parable, where an excess of savings over investment in the *Treatise* sense was associated with a continuous fall in prices and money wages, or efficiency earnings, until the excess of savings over investment is somehow eliminated or "...all production cease and the entire population starves to death" (JMK, V, 158–60). The multiplier analysis was used in the Easter Term 1932 (Rymes, 1986) lectures to ensure stability of prices and money wages but also to demonstrate that upward and downward movements in the levels of prices and money earnings would not necessarily rule out the possibility of the equilibration of investment and consumption occurring at less than a full employment equilibrium.

In the 1933 lectures the multiplier is more connected with changes in the quantities of investment, consumption and output, where the movements of prices are, in the analysis, more suppressed. It should be remembered, though, that it is essential to Keynes's analysis, that, given money wages, the prices of investment and consumption goods be free to move. It is through the higher prices of new capital goods, associated with lower rates of interest, that higher levels of real capital formation, i.e., a greater supply of new capital goods, are brought about and, through the multiplier, a greater volume of new consumption goods, *associated with a higher price of such consumption goods*, is created. Without the higher price of capital goods and consumption goods, the Kahn multiplier is not underway, unless recourse is had to less than perfectly competitive assumptions associated with constant marginal costs of production in the new capital and consumptions goods industries.[14]

Thus, a second source of potential confusion in the minds of his students and, consequently, in the lecture notes, is that the investment-savings mechanism was being switched from the determination of the level of prices to the level of quantities with a continued examination of the stability associated with movements in money wages or efficiency earnings.

The realization that students of Keynes's lectures would be confronted with the need to be aware of tumultuous and far-reaching theoretical arguments is the major problem I confronted in transcribing the original notes and constructing the notes of a representative student. I refer again to the user cost as an illustration. Tarshis, whose notes provide the basic foundation for the synthesis, provides extensive notes on this concept. Bryce does not. Which notetaker correctly reflected Keynes's own emphasis, the importance which Keynes himself attached to the concept? Were Keynes's lectures on user cost

14/ Kahn's own discussion of his multiplier would indicate that an important component in his own thinking was the determination of the level of prices other than through the quantity theory of money (letter to D. Patinkin, 19 March 1974 in Patinkin & Leith 1977, 147). See also the preface to the French edition of the *General Theory* (JMK, VII, xxxiv–v).

fundamental and should every reference, every scrap, be woven into the representative synthesis? Were the lectures misplaced, was the concept a red herring and therefore is it correct in any synthesis to rely more heavily on those notes in which only scant references to the concept appear?

The construction of the synthesis cannot be done in a vacuum. Once the transcribed notes are to hand, considerable repetition requires that a synthesis, the notes of a representative student, be prepared. The editor of such a synthesis must have a view as to the lecturer's major concerns. My view was that Keynes was first and foremost a monetary theorist, attempting to do what he claimed, namely, to set out a monetary theory of value. No observation of importance from the raw material of the transcribed notes has been consciously missed in the synthesis. Where points are made in the notes which are on the major development of Keynes' thought, however, I have tried to present, even running the risk of repetition, all the points available in the notes. I have tried to construct the synthesis without comment, I have reported confusions and contradictions without editorial reflection but I have tried to make the synthesis or representative notes as full as economically possible because of the view I hold that Keynes in the 1930s was engaged in a large enterprise, that is, the construction of a general equilibrium monetary theory of value.

History of the Lecture Notes

It was happenstance which caused me to undertake this endeavour to construct a representative student's notes of Keynes's lectures in the period 1932 to 1935.

Here are the names of students' notes, in terms of the years in which they attended Keynes's Cambridge lectures in the Michaelmas term, which form my raw material. (Minor observations about this list, such as, for instance, the last few pages of Hopkin's notes would seem to pertain to 1935, must be noted.)

Notes by:	1932	1933	1934	1935
Robert B. Bryce	x	x	x	
Alec Cairncross	x	x		
D. G. Champernowne			x	
M. Fallgatter		x		
Bryan Hopkin			x	
Lorie Tarshis	x	x	x	x
Walter Salant		x		
Bryn Thring		x	x	

I asked Bryce when we were at the University of Western Ontario's Conference on Keynes in the fall of 1975 if he would be kind enough to deposit his original lecture notes with the Rare Book Collection of the MacOdrum Library at Carleton University. He did. An examination of the notes revealed that a transcription would be useful to interested scholars. Later in the Fall Term of 1977 while I was on sabbatical leave at the University of Chicago, Professor Don Patinkin, also on sabbatical leave from the Hebrew University of Jerusalem, not only encouraged me to complete my transcription of Bryce's notes but also gave me copies of a collation of a typewritten version of the lecture notes by Bryce and Professor Lorie Tarshis, then at Scarborough College of the University of Toronto, which Patinkin had prepared. I later obtained xerox copies of Tarshis' original hand written notes (which are now with the Keynes papers in King's College Library at Cambridge).

Later at Carleton in the Fall Term 1979, Bryce was kind enough to come out on Friday mornings to the Carleton Library to read over his notes with me and to give me as well some sense of the initial puzzlement and then growing excitement of the times he spent listening to Keynes not only in his lectures but at the Monday evening meetings of Keynes's Political Economy Club. I tried to ensure that Bryce's reading of his notes and my transcription of them which he checked did not 'correct' the notes on the basis of knowledge subsequently gained.

Tarshis was kind enough to go over his original notes with me in April 1980 and later answered questions I had on the basis of a first transcription in the Summer of 1983. He kindly commented on, and made emendations to, a draft transcription of his notes in 1984, prepared while I was on sabbatical leave at the Australian National University in Canberra.

Professor Donald Moggridge supplied me with xerox copies of the notes by Thring and Champernowne. I was able to check the Thring notes thanks to Judith Allen while I was at Cambridge in Michaelmas Term 1985. The original Champernowne notes have, alas, been destroyed. All that remains available is the xerox copy of his notes for the year 1934 in the Keynes Papers in King's College Library which Moggridge had supplied.

Dr. Walter Salant, Senior Fellow Emeritus, The Brookings Institution, kindly supplied me with a copy of his notes for 1933 and corrected my first draft of them in 1985.

Through Professor Patinkin and Professor James Early, Department of Economics, University of California, Riverside, I secured a copy of the typescript of the notes taken by Marvin Fallgatter, a physicist who, at Cambridge, went to Keynes's lectures in 1933, took notes and then typed them. These notes were sent by Fallgatter to Early, who roomed with Fallgatter at Antioch College in 1926 and were used by Early as a graduate student at Wisconsin in 1935. Professor Early kindly checked my transcription of the Fallgatter notes.

With the help of Dr. Geoff Harcourt, I obtained xerox copies of notes for 1934 from Sir Bryan Hopkin. He also extensively and kindly commented on the transcriptions I made while I was in Australia.

Sir Austin Robinson obtained and passed along to me the xerox copies of the notes taken by Sir Alec Cairncross for 1932 and 1933. Sir Alec commented on two transcriptions I made of his notes, written again while I was at Australian National University.

These are, then, the notes that I have been successful in unearthing. Sir Austin Robinson kindly arranged the following note to be published in the *Economic Journal* (XCV, March 1985, 282):

> Professor T.K. Rymes of Carleton University, Ottawa, Canada, has for some time past been collecting the lecture notes of students who attended lectures by Keynes during the period between the publication of *A Treatise on Money* and the publication of the *General Theory*. A number of sets of lecture notes have already been received. At present the intention is to transcribe these and hold the transcripts of the notes in one or two places, including the Keynes archive in Cambridge. If any person who attended lectures by Keynes in Cambridge during these years has a set of lecture notes the editors or Professor Rymes would be most interested to hear from them.

So far there has been no response. In addition a large number of people were written to: almost all who received firsts and some who received seconds in Part II of the Economics Tripos in 1933, 1934, 1935 and 1936. Though many letters of encouragement were received, it was invariably the case that the writer had not taken notes, or, if he had, they had been destroyed in World War II, had been lost or, sad to say, had been thrown away or stolen! Some of the comments in the letters are of interest. For instance:

> ...I fear I cannot help you. In any case, Keynes had a

habit of contradicting in one lecture what he had said at some earlier time, which certainly added to one's interest in economic theory, but confused one's notes. I fancy there was also considerable confusion in the answers given during the Tripos, between pre-Keynes, early Keynes and the latest Keynes!

And

Incidentally, quite a number of people used to come from London to attend his lectures, and the atmosphere was one of a public performance rather than of academic discourse. He himself regarded them as "putting across" his ideas.

I do not wish to be too discouraging, but in view of this, I doubt whether any notes which might have been preserved (presumably there are none of his own, as he didn't have any) will add much to [the] understanding of the development of his ideas.

And

I did indeed attend Keynes's lectures for the period he gave them. He introduced the series by saying: "I have been giving this series of lectures for the last ten years, and am proud to say that I have never repeated myself, neither have I ever finished the series" (or words to that effect).

True enough: He stopped about half way through the year [sic]. I found him spell-binding as a personality and utterly charming, but I fear most of what he said was well over my head....

It was not until his book on the Theory of Employment

came out a few years later that I realised I had been listening to it in embryo.

And a former student was told at his third supervision in 1932:

> You seem to be literate. Read the *Economics of Welfare* as well as Marshall. Don't bother to go to lectures. But go to Keynes's.

With the transcriptions of the Bryce, Cairncross, Champernowne, Fallgatter, Hopkin, Tarshis, Salant and Thring notes assembled, the question was "What should be done with them?" I have done two things: (i) a typescript volume of all the transcriptions has been prepared. It is called *Keynes's Lectures, 1932–34: Notes of Students*; (ii) I have edited a volume called *Keynes's Lectures' 1932–35: Notes of a Representative Student*. This volume, as its title, based on the Marshallian conception of a representative or average firm, would suggest,[15] is a synthesis of the transcriptions.

To be precise, because one of the set of notes, those of Tarshis, runs through the entire period, *Notes of a Representative Student* are built around it. I have, however, continuously referred to and introduced elements from the other sets of notes where there was emphatic agreement amongst all the topics and where there were different interpretations, different emphases, notation and particularly where there were gaps in the Tarshis notes.

The notetakers had diverse backgrounds. Tarshis was a trained economist.[16] Indeed, when he took Keynes's lectures

---

15/ I am indebted to Professor Patinkin for discussions as to whether the title should refer to *a* or *the* representative student. In Marshall's *Principles of Economics*, there are references to both a and the representative or average firm.

16/ He had academic training in economics in the Department of Political in 1932 he was confused because he had made an intensive investment in the *Treatise*. He would naturally focus, therefore, on those elements of Keynes's lectures which were of a theoretical nature. Bryce was an engineer who, upon arriving in Cambridge after graduation from the University of Toronto, had no formal training in economics and was always more interested in the policy implications of Keynes's analysis (Bryce 1985, 1939). Cairncross and Champernowne were research students. Champernowne in particular had an interest in mathematics, achieving a first in Parts I and II of the Mathematics Tripos. He subsequently published one of the more mathematical statements of Keynes's *General Theory* (Champernowne 1936). Indeed, Champernowne's published diagrams and equations can easily be cast in ISLM terms – so he must be regarded, along with Hicks, Reddaway and Meade, as one of the original formalizers of Keynes's *General Theory*. Salant went on to a distinguished career in academic economics while Hopkin and Thring pursued work in the U.K. public service. Fallgatter, of whom little is known, brought a physics training to his rendition of Keynes's lectures.

There is then a considerable diversity of backgrounds and interests in the notetakers. There are, as well, differences in the notes. Bryce's and Tarshis's are primarily their recording of what was said in the lectures, though there are marginalia which indicate later additions, queries and comments. It will be remembered that Tarshis and Bryce were friends, did cross reference their notes and on one occasion at least Tarshis copied Bryce's notes for a lecture he apparently missed. The Cairncross, Salant and Thring notes appear to be standard student's notes, taken independently without later reconsideration and subsequent emendation. Champernowne's are brief

Economy at the University of Toronto under Wynne Plumptre, Vincent Bladen, Harry Cassidy, Donald McGregor, Harold Innis and E.J. Urwick (Harcourt 1982 and correspondence with Tarshis, October 1986).

and succinct (curiously with cartoon portraiture of Keynes the 'Master') as one would expect from his *Review of Economic Studies* statement. Fallgatter's were typed and sent to Early – how much editing and emendation occurred when Fallgatter constructed the typed version is not known. Hopkin's notes are a carefully reworked and even meticulously paginated version of what Keynes said and so cannot be considered as "spontaneous" as the others. Thus, added to the diversity of the backgrounds of the notetakers is the diversity of the notes themselves.

Following the advice of Sir Desmond Lee and Professor Donald Moggridge I have *never* "corrected" the notes based on subsequent understandings of the *General Theory*. Where the notes are confused, where the notation appears to be different as distinct from in error, etc., I have allowed them to stand, though not necessarily unremarked. Keynes changed his mind, reformulated again and over again his thoughts and analysis. To the extent that the lecture notes reflect digressions, false starts etc., on the way to the *General Theory*, then the notes add to our understanding of the development of Keynes's ideas.

An Exemplary Treatment: 1933

To the extent that Tarshis's and Bryce's notes are 'independent', I have three independent observations for 1932, six for 1933, five for 1934 and essentially only one for 1935. (The presumption that Hopkin's notes extended into 1935 has been noted.) I may be useful if I elaborate then more fully on the *Notes of a Representative Student* for 1933.

It is first noted that Tarshis did not have a title in his notes, nor did Bryce and Cairncross but the title "The Monetary Theory of Production" appears in Fallgatter,[17] Salant and

17/ Fallgatter apparently missed the first lecture, as did Cairncross. For

Thring. Tarshis starts by pointing out that the framework of the *Treatise*, i.e., [Marshallian] momentary (or temporary) equilibrium analysis, can be shifted away from the determination of the level of money prices of the volume of output and employment. Bryce adds that the determination of the level of money prices is not an interesting thing, except to the debtor class. The notes describe how classical economists were largely concerned with the distribution of a *given* (the underlining appears in Salant) volume of resources between different uses. But the notes also indicate confusion as to who were designated as classical economists since it is reported that they were also concerned with the question of what determined the *volume* (the underlining appears in Tarshis) of employed resources. Bryce has Keynes stating that it is awfully hard to find a definite statement of the classical approach to the volume of employment.

There is an extensive discussion in the notes of the demand and supply schedules for labour. In Bryce's notes, the important observation is made that not only does "the" intersection of the two schedules determine the level of employment but classical theory says the level of total output is also determined and goes on to determine the composition and distribution of that output. Certain types of unemployment were described as voluntary. There is, however, a pronounced and obvious lack of clarity which may have arisen because, Tarshis said, Keynes went at such a pace that he feared he had copied imprecisely. Bryce as well commented on the speed with which Keynes lectured on what was apparently a favourite subject. I have, therefore, expanded the notes at this stage to give as many of the statements as possible.

In Bryce, Salant and Thring's notes, the definitions of involuntary unemployment are exactly the same and are

statement concerning the changes Keynes made to the title of his course of lectures see JMK, VII, xvi.

virtually the same as in Tarshis. Keynes had the classical supply schedule as wrong since he interprets it as saying that the real wage rate equals the marginal disutility of that *equilibrium* amount of employment. The word equilibrium appears in Tarshis, whereas in Bryce, the argument is that the real wage equals the marginal disutility of a given volume of employment. The notes I have prepared draw extensively here on all four students but Salant summarizes when he says that if involuntary unemployment in Keynes's sense exists then the second classical postulate is wrong. One must make a new analysis, says Salant, rather than applying equilibrium-type reasoning to non-equilibrium situations. Again I emphasize how extensive my representative notes are at this point. Why? Though I make no such suggestion in my notes, it is clear that the notetakers presage the work of Patinkin and Clower (Patinkin 1965 and Clower 1965). This is illustrated by the references in the notes to the classical theorists being likened to Euclidean geometers in a non-Euclidean world.

By the second lecture of 1933, Fallgatter and Cairncross are apparently in attendance and the observations are correspondingly richer. I bring in references by them as soon as possible since I want to capture the representative observations of yet another research student and an interested lay person.

The notes of the second lecture are replete with references to Co-operative economies, Neutral economies and Entrepreneur or Money-Wage economies, a classification scheme which Keynes abandoned in the *General Theory*. Again, I have recorded such observations extensively since the classification system is important in the overriding theme set out above (Torr 1980). Cairncross notes, for instance, that money is introduced by classical economists into Neutral economies merely as a convenience. At this point as well, Keynes made extensive references to Marx.

The third lecture carries on with extensive discussions of the Entrepreneur Economy, Neutral economies and of 'hoarding'. In certain instances, some of the notes (e.g., Bryce's) become simultaneously extensive but sketchy, at which time I again relied upon more extensive references.

The fourth lecture opens with much discussion of methodology, philosophy and scholasticism. It is interesting that Salant takes no note of Keynes's extensive discourse on methodology while Thring refers to it parenthetically. The discussion is important because as the notes reveal it leads up to Keynes's very extensive discussions about *expectations*. It becomes clear from such extensive references that Keynes was grappling with difficult problems indeed.

In the fifth lecture, the notetakers reflect Keynes's great trouble with definitions of income, and how clear it was beginning to be. Most notes refer now to Aggregate Disbursement equal, in equilibrium, to "Yncome". Even formal relations appear, e.g.

$$Y = E + Q = C + I = D$$

and $Y = E + Q = C + S$

Extensive cross referencing among the notes of the difference between the comparative freedom of the individual to have disbursement differ from income and the necessary equality for the community as a whole is undertaken. The notes emphasize that it is both *prices and incomes* which equilibrate disbursements and income or which bring investment and savings into equality. The notes reflect fully the references to prices and incomes because they here indicate the basic fact that Keynes's momentary equilibria entailed the simultaneous determination of prices and quantities (i.e., equilibrium nominal income), a blending of the analysis of the *Treatise* and the *General Theory*.

To quote from the notes:

The income and price system is a determinand not a

determinar – it must bring itself into adjustment. This is one of the most fundamental features of monetary systems.

Some idea of Keynes's lecturing style is obtained from Fallgatter's notes when the sixth lecture begins with Keynes quoted as saying:

I have so far given you mainly symbols and definitions and truisms, which are rather barren of content. In this lecture I shall try to give you much of the real substance of my remarks, and shall rather rush through to my conclusions.

In the seventh lecture, when Keynes is discussing Kahn's multiplier, the notes of the various students, in setting out the formula, sometimes employ total derivatives, sometimes partial derivatives and sometimes discrete notation. That is, the increment of employment, N_1, in the consumption goods industries is sometimes written as dN_1, ∂N_1 and ΔN_1. In Tarshis's notes, there are marginalia (it is not known if the marginalia were written at the time of the notetaking) likening the multiplier to an infinite geometric progression, seeming to confirm Keynes's understanding of the stability properties of the multiplier process. Even more significantly, at this point k, the multiplier, is indicated in the notes as ranging between 1 and infinity. Both Cairncross and Fallgatter note that if k $= \infty$, then an "...inauguration of a public works program would induce an *unlimited* rise in prices". This is important to record because the notes therefore indicate that Keynes continues in 1933 the use of the multiplier to determine equilibrium *prices* and quantities and hence aggregate money income.

   In the notes on the determination of investment, the notes of Cairncross, Fallgatter and Salant refer explicitly to considerations of risk differences in discount formulae. All the notes attest vividly to the importance of uncertainty in Keynes's theory of investment.

The notes for the eighth and final lecture for Michaelmas 1933 confirm that Keynes had fully worked out the liquidity preference theory of the rate of interest, even to the point of Fallgatter noting that if prices are expected to rise (fall), there will be a decrease (increase) in the demand for money.

In this lecture, in almost all the notes we find

$$M = A(W, \rho)$$

where $A(W, \rho)$ is the demand for money to hold in relation to income and is expressed as a function of the state of the news, W, and the rate of interest, ρ with M being the stock supply of money.

All the notes concentrate on the three determinants of the rate of interest, A, liquidity preference, itself a function of the state of the news, W and the quantity of money, M - i.e., A, W and M as being exogenous. Again, the notes reflect the continued inference of Keynes that expressions such as $M = A(W, \rho)$ are not formal relationships (for instance, modern questions would be: how to measure W and does it relate positively or negatively to the demand for money?) but rather a method of thought. The listeners were sometimes disconcerted by such philosophical suggestions from Keynes. In Tarshis's notes at this point we find: "What the Hell".

The lecture concluded on Keynes's view of the future of capitalism. Strangely enough, Fallgatter's notes are the most dramatic. His notes stress the need for the *evaporation* of the rate of interest (there is no mention of the euthanasia of the rentier in other notes), the idea that the inability of the interest rate to fall has brought down empires and Keynes saying that, if his views are correct, all past teaching has been either irrelevant or else positively injurious. Is it just an accident that the more flamboyant, controversial and dramatic Keynes was captured by Fallgatter, essentially a visitor to the economics domain? Did the other notetakers hold back for some reason? Was it Keynes; or just Fallgatter? One cannot say.

The example for 1933 illustrates all too briefly just how difficult it is to construct *Notes of a Representative Student*. However, they faithfully reflect, I believe, what the students heard (or thought) Keynes to be saying.

Two final points should be made. Wherever possible, I have given references Keynes's writings and those of others when the notes themselves refer to them. In the notes for 1933, for example, one pays attention to the discussion among Robertson, Hawtrey and Keynes about saving and hoarding which took place in the *Economic Journal* that year. Such evidence is helpful in interpreting the notes but not necessarily in reconstructing them which is my task. It does not necessarily follow, from what we know of Keynes's lecturing style, that what was said in the lectures corresponds with what was published either before or after the lectures.

The notes display all the characteristics of students' other preoccupations. Romantic couplets adorn some of the pages, scribblings in the margin indicate that minds were elsewhere than in the lecture hall in the Arts School and caricatures of Keynes himself sometimes found in the notes indicate that students may have found fascination in the style of delivery and the presence and personality of Keynes and were not necessarily at all times absorbed in the foundations of the economic theory the "Master" was presenting.

Conclusion

How does one edit notes taken by students of lectures? Two things should be done. First, a transcription of the lecture notes, which is faithful to every detail, should be undertaken. That transcription is in *Keynes's Lectures, 1932–35: Notes of*

Students, wherein I indicate every misspelling, every shorthand, every incorrect notation, every gap and so forth. In short, in the transcription, I have followed Tanselle's advice (Tanselle, 1979, 497):

> In the case of note-books, diaries, letters, and the like, [no mention is made of lecture notes] whatever state they are in constitutes their finished form, and the question of whether the notes "intended" something else is irrelevant...if he [the editor] presents them as anything more polished or finished than they were left by the writer, he is falsifying their nature.

A synthesis, *Keynes's Lectures, 1932–35: Notes of a Representative Student*, has been prepared because the transcriptions are repetitive[18] and need to be boiled down to a representative statement. Here, as editor, I have tried to reflect what the students believed, as indicated by their notes, Keynes was saying. I have tried to make the representation faithful but I stress the difficulties. Keynes was working on a general monetary theory of value. Some students perceived this, at least partially (e.g. Tarshis), others hardly reflected this at all. A general theory was Keynes's preoccupation – this is the theme which lies behind the synthesis. It is clearly necessary for an editor to have a theory about what the students were hearing and attempting to understand and to record. I have allowed Keynes's concern with a general monetary theory of

---

18/ Drake (1980) writes of editorial screening with an eye to economic realities and scholarly utility. Curiously in none of the volumes of the Conference on Editorial Problems is there an essay dealing with the problem of editing students' notes. In economics, I know of at least two cases where students' notes have been edited into textbooks, but only after the direct or indirect examination of the text by the lecturer himself (Friedman 1962; Johnson 1971).

value to be that theory. That view has played the sole role, not of selecting material for the synthesis in which faithfulness to the transcriptions is sought, but rather of providing a guide as to when to expand the synthesis. If one student's notes make little mention of user cost while another's are replete with extensive references, then, given the editor's theory of what was the concern of the lectures, the extensive references are used, though the lack of unanimity is noted.

The notes are used by scholars to 'date' Keynes's ideas (Patinkin 1976; Clarke 1985) and to arrange related materials (Moggridge 1973; JMK, XIII). The synthetic notes should be as representative and as exhaustive as possible, however, to reflect the false starts, the confusions, the theoretical meanderings which characterize Keynes's attempts to construct a general monetary theory of value – one manifestation of which is the *General Theory*. If the synthesis helps to capture as well the tumult of ideas which is associated with the Keynesian revolution, then they will have served a useful purpose.

Works Cited

Bensusan-Butt, David 1980, *On Economic Knowledge: A Skeptical Miscellany*, Canberra: Australian National University Press.

Brown, A.J. 1987, "A Worm's View of the Keynesian Revolution", in J. Hillard (ed.), *John Maynard Keynes in Retrospect*, Upleadon: Edward Elgar.

Bryce, Robert B. 1934, "An Introduction to Monetary Theory of Employment", a paper presented at Professor Hayek's seminar at the London School of Economics, Spring-Summer, in JMK, XXIX, 132–5; Patinkin & Leith 1977, Appendix 1.

—, 1939, "The Effects on Canada of Industrial Fluctuations in the United States", *Canadian Journal of Economics and Political Science*, V (August), 373–86.

—, 1977, "Keynes as Seen by His Students in the 1930s", in Patinkin & Leith 1977.

Champernowne, D.G. 1936, "Unemployment, Basic and Monetary: The Classical Analysis and the Keynesian", *Review of Economic Studies*, III (June), 201–16.

Clarke, P.F. 1986, "Keynes's General Theory: A Problem for Historians", mimeo, October.

Clower, Robert W. 1965, "The Keynesian Counter-revolution: A Theoretical Appraisal" in Walker 1984.

Drake, Stillman 1982, "Dating Unpublished Notes, such as Gallileo's on Motion", in Levere 1982.

Durbin, Elizabeth 1985, *New Jerusalems: The Labour Party and the Economics of Democratic Socialism*, London: Routledge & Kegan Paul.

Eshag, Eprime 1963, *From Marshall to Keynes: An Essay in the Monetary Theory of the Cambridge School*, Oxford: Blackwell.

Friedman, Milton 1962, *Price Theory: A Provisional Text*, Chicago: Aldine.

Friedman, Milton & Schwartz, Anna J. 1963, *A Monetary History of the United States, 1867–1960*, Princeton: Princeton University Press.

Harcourt, G.C. 1982, "An Early Post-Keynesian: Lorie Tarshis (or: Tarshis on Tarshis by Harcourt)", *Journal of Post-Keynesian Economics*, IV (Summer), 609–19.

Johnson, Elizabeth and Harry G. 1978, *The Shadow of Keynes: Understanding Keynes, Cambridge and Keynesian Economics*, Oxford: Blackwell.

Johnson, Harry G. 1971, *Macroeconomics and Monetary Theory*, London: Gray-Mills.

— 1976, "Keynes's *General Theory*: Revolution or War of Independence", *Canadian Journal of Economics*, IX (November), 580–94, reprinted in Johnson, Elizabeth and Harry G. 1978.

Kahn, Richard 1929, *The Economics of the Short Period*, Fellowship dissertation submitted to King's College, Cambridge.

— 1984, *The Making of Keynes's General Theory*, Cambridge: Cambridge University Press.

Keynes, John Maynard 1971–, *The Collected Writings of John Maynard Keynes*, (eds. E. Johnson and D. Moggridge), 29 vols., London: Macmillan.

Keynes, Milo (ed.) 1975, *Essays on John Maynard Keynes*, Cambridge: Cambridge University Press.

Kregel, Jan 1985, "Hamlet without the Prince: Cambridge Macroeconomics without Money", *American Economic Review*, LXXC (May), 133–9.

Lawson, T. & Pesaran, H. (eds.) 1985, *Keynes' Economics: Methodological Issues*, London: Croom Helm.

Lee, Sir Desmond (ed.), *Wittenstein's Lectures, Cambridge 1930– 1936: From the Notes of John King and Desmond Lee*, Oxford: Blackwell.

Levere, Trevor (ed.) 1982, *Editing Texts in the History of Science and Medicine*, New York: Garland.

Moggridge, D.E. 1972, *British Monetary Policy 1924–1931: The Norman Conquest of $4.86*, Cambridge: Cambridge University Press.

— 1973, "From the Treatise to the General Theory: An Exercise in Chronology", *History of Political Economy*, V (Spring), 72–88.

Patinkin, D. 1965, *Money, Interest and Prices*, 2nd ed., New York: Harper and Row.

— 1976, *Keynes' Monetary Thought: A Study of its Development*, Durham: Duke University Press.

— 1982, *Anticipations of the General Theory and Other Essays on Keynes*, Chicago: University of Chicago Press.

Patinkin, D. & Leith, J.C. (eds.) 1977, *Keynes, Cambridge and the General Theory: The Process of Criticism and Discussion Connected with the Development of the General Theory*, London: Macmillan.

Plumptre, A.F.W. 1947, "Keynes in Cambridge", *Canadian Journal of Economics and Political Science*, XIII (August), 366–71.

— 1975, "Maynard Keynes as a Teacher", in Milo Keynes (1975).

Robertson, D.H. 1926, *Banking Policy and the Price Level*, London: P.S. King.

Robinson, Joan 1933a, "A Parable on Saving and Investment", *Economica*, XIII (February), 75–84.

— 1933b, *The Economics of Imperfect Competition*, London: Macmillan.

Rymes, T.K., "Keynes's Lectures, 1932–35: Notes of a Representative Student. A Prelude: Notes for the Easter Term 1932", *Eastern Economic Journal*, XII (October–December), 397–412.

Salant, Walter S. 1977, "Keynes as Seen by his Students in the 1930s", in Patinkin & Leith 1977.

Shackle, G.L.S. 1967, *The Years of High Theory: Invention and Tradition in Economic Thought, 1926–1939*, Cambridge: Cambridge University Press.

Smith, Vera Constance 1936, *The Rationale of Central Banking*, London: P.S. King.

Tanselle, G. Thomas 1979, "The Editing of Historical Documents", *Studies in Bibliography*, XXXI, 1–96 reprinted in his *Selected Studies in Bibliography*, Charlottesville: University Press of Virginia.

Tarshis, Lorie 1975, "A Review of *The Collected Writings of John Maynard Keynes*, XIII and XXIV", *Journal of Economic Literature*, XIV (December), 1282–6.

— 1977, "Keynes as Seen by his Students in the 1930s", in Patinkin & Leith (1977).

— 1979, "The Aggregate Supply Function in Keynes's General Theory" in *Economics and Welfare: Essays in Honour of Tibor Scitovsky*, London: Academic Press.

Townshend, H. 1937, "Liquidity-premium and the Theory of Value", *Economic Journal*, XLVII (March), 157–69.

Torr, C.S.W. 1980, "The Distinction Between an Entrepreneur Economy and a Co-operative Economy: A Review Note", *South African Journal of Economics*, XLVIII (December), 429–34.

Walker, D. (ed.) 1984, *Money and Markets: Essays by Robert W. Clower*, Cambridge: Cambridge University Press.

von Hayek, F.A. 1931, *Prices and Production*, London: Routledge & Sons.

Economists as Policy-Makers: Editing the Papers of James Meade, Lionel Robbins, and The Economic Advisory Council*

Susan Howson

The Economic Advisory Council of the 1930s represents the first peacetime involvement of professional economists in British government policy-making. It was the forerunner of the government's Economic Section, in which Robbins and Meade both gained experience of policy-making, during the

*My editorial work has been assisted at various times by the Social Science Research Council of the UK, the Social Sciences and Humanities Research Council of Canada, the Humanities and Social Sciences Committee of the Research Board of the University of Toronto, and the Wincott Foundation. I should also like to thank Professor Meade, Lady Robbins, Dr. Angela Raspin of the British Library of Political and Economic Science, Dr. Stephen Bird of the Labour Party, and the Controller of Her Majesty's Stationery Office for permission to use the documents discussed in this paper, and Donald Moggridge and the other participants in the 22nd Conference on Editorial Problems for their comments and questions, some of which I hope I have answered in this paper.

Second World War and in the immediate postwar years. I shall therefore begin this paper by outlining the work of the Economic Advisory Council (EAC) and of Meade and Robbins in the wartime Economic Section, before discussing the editorial problems of their papers. After describing my experiences in editing the papers of the EAC, James Meade and, to a lesser extent, Lionel Robbins, I shall conclude with a few remarks on their role in the development of economic policy-making in Britain.

Economists had been drawn into British government service during the First World War but it was not until James Ramsay MacDonald, the first Labour Prime Minister, in his second administration established the Economic Advisory Council with its many committees and full-time secretariat in 1930 that economists were intended to contribute to policy-making as economists and on a permanent basis. (Sir Ralph Hawtrey's occupation in the Treasury, as the so-called Director of Financial Enquiries from 1919 until the end of the Second World War, is not an exception to this statement since Hawtrey was not a professional economist.) The Council itself was composed of businessmen and trade union leaders as well as economists; it initially met monthly but quickly degenerated into a talking shop, meeting only three times in 1931 and only once after the 1931 financial crisis. By this time, however, a standing Committee on Economic Information had joined the fifteen other committees appointed in 1930 and 1931 to consider specific topics. Its terms of reference were "to supervise the preparation of monthly reports ...on the economic situation and to advise as to the continuous study of economic development". This committee continued to meet regularly and survived until September 1939. The economists most involved in the work of the EAC and its more important committees, particularly the Committee on Economic Information, were Hubert Henderson, the full-time secretary of the Council, J.M. Keynes, Colin Clark (a junior member of the Council staff) and D.H. Robertson from 1936. (Also Josiah Stamp but you may not want to call him an economist.)[1]

The approach of war in the later 1930s revived the Committee on Economic Information which had been in danger of disappearing through inactivity in early 1938. In addition to preparing two important reports on the economic problems of rearmament, economists on the Committee on Economic Information were called upon to advise on the preparations for a war economy and the financing of the war effort, with economists serving on Treasury committees and Josiah Stamp, Hubert Henderson and Henry Clay (Economic Adviser to the Bank of England) appointed to prepare a "survey of war plans in the economic and financial sphere" in the summer of 1939. After the outbreak of war the Stamp Survey was provided with a staff of economists and statisticians, which included John Jewkes and Austin Robinson (the original members), Lionel Robbins, James Meade and Richard Stone. This "Central Economic Information Service", with further additions of personnel, was split into the Central Statistical Office and the Economic Section of the War Cabinet Offices in January 1941. Meanwhile, Keynes, Henderson and Robertson joined the Treasury for the duration (and other economists served in the Board of Trade and other government departments). The Economic Section remained in the Cabinet Offices in the early postwar years but it was subsequently taken over by the Treasury in and after 1947.

Lionel Robbins was first involved in this story of economists as policy-makers in Britain when he was the youngest member of a Committee of Economists of the Economic Advisory Council set up with Keynes as chairman

1/ This paragraph and the next are based on Howson and Winch 1977, Hopkins 1951, Chester 1951, and Wilson 1975, paras. 965–970. Further information on the individuals mentioned is given in the appendix to this paper.

in 1930 to analyse the economic problems of that year and how to solve them. The other members besides Keynes were Henderson, Stamp and A.C. Pigou with Richard Kahn as one of the secretaries. Robbins was then the recently appointed Professor of Economics at the London School of Economics (LSE), and achieved some notoriety in challenging Keynes and refusing to sign a report which allowed both protection and public works as possible remedies for some British unemployment. Robbins wrote of this episode in his autobiography (I quote sparingly):

> ...alas, when the report came to be drafted, I found that it was expected that I should agree with recommendations with two of which I was in sharp disagreement.... [T]hese were not issues on which I found myself able to compromise or to acquiesce...in having my dissent recorded in brackets embodied in an argument which tended entirely in the opposite direction; nothing but a separate document giving a reasoned statement for my attitude would suffice. Keynes...was furious. ... He denounced me before the others and laid it down that, as a minority of one, I was not entitled to a separate report. This was very distressing for me. ... But, rightly or wrongly, my conscience was involved and I was not prepared to give way... [Eventually] Keynes capitulated. ... It was intimated, however, that my presence was no longer desired at the final meeting of the committee. (Robbins 1971, 150–2; see also Howson and Winch 1977, 46–72 and 180–243).

Robbins reappears in the story in 1940 when he was recruited into the Central Economic Information Service. When the economists and statisticians were separated Jewkes became the first Director of the Economic Section; Robbins soon took over from him, relinquishing the position at the end of 1945 when he returned to academic life and LSE. His successor was James Meade.

I have already mentioned Meade as one of the economists who joined the Central Economic Information Service in 1940. He and his family had recently escaped from France ahead of the invading German army, on their way from Geneva where he had been working for the League of Nations (as an economist) since December 1937 (Meade 1977).[2] His activities as an adviser on economic policy go back, however, to 1933, when he was the first of a group of Oxford economists to be consulted on the formation of a suitable economic and financial policy for a future majority Labour government by Hugh Dalton, later Chancellor of the Exchequer in the first majority Labour government in 1945. Dalton passed on many of Meade's ideas to the policy committee of the National Executive Committee of the Party (Durbin 1985, 97–8, 114, 210–14, 216, 220; Howson 1986, 4–5). When Meade entered government service he decided to behave exactly as a civil servant without engaging in political activity,[3] so that his work for the Labour Party was produced in the mid-1930s and in and after 1948. He stayed with the Section, as Director from January 1946, until he became Professor of Commerce with special reference to International Trade at the London School of Economics in the autumn of 1947. It was at LSE that he produced his work on the theory of the balance of payments which earned him the Nobel Prize for Economics for 1977 (Meade 1951 and 1955). But his work in the Section had been equally pathbreaking – I shall use his own characteristically modest words to summarise his activities there:

First and foremost in 1940 and 1941 Richard Stone and I prepared the first official estimates of the UK national

2/ I have included this account by Meade of his life in Meade 1987.
3/ Meade to Howson, 12 May 1986.

income and expenditure, and we did so in a form which constituted what was, I believe, the first true double-entry social accounts prepared for any country. Second, there were the discussions and drafts leading up to the White Paper on Employment Policy of 1944, in which the UK government accepted the maintenance of employment as an obligation of governmental policy. Third, there were the discussions, state papers and conferences leading up to the post-war international economic and financial settlement, namely the International Monetary Fund, the International Bank for Reconstruction and Development and the General Agreement on Tariffs and Trade. I was especially concerned with the last of these. (Meade 1977)

If Meade were not so modest, he could have said that in 1942 he wrote "a proposal for an international commercial union" to complement Keynes's "clearing union" plan. This became, and remained, the basis of the charter for an International Trade Organisation drafted at the United Nations Conference on Trade and Employment in London in October 1946. Although the ITO Charter was not ratified, its principles were incorporated in the GATT rules agreed at Geneva in 1947.[4] Of Meade's work as Director of the postwar Section I shall have something more to say later.

* * *

Now that I have provided you with a potted history of the Economic Advisory Council and of the Economic Section in which both Robbins and Meade were employed, let me

4/ EC(S)(42)19, "A proposal for an international commercial union", 28 July 1942, PRO T230/14; Gardner 1956, chapters 6, 8, 14 and 17. It should also be noted that for the development of national income accounting Stone was awarded the Nobel Memorial Prize in Economics in 1984. On Meade's role in employment policy see also below pp. 144–5.

turn to the *editorial problems* associated with these bodies. First of all, *the nature of the surviving records.* Since the EAC, the Committee on Economic Information, and the other EAC committees were part of or served by the Cabinet Secretariat their records are among the Cabinet Office records in the Public Record Office (PRO) in London, while the Economic Section's records, reflecting its ultimate location in Whitehall, are in the Treasury papers in the PRO (classes CAB58 and T230 respectively). There also exist the private papers of several major participants, including MacDonald, Keynes, and Henderson as well as Robbins and Meade. In addition, Meade's work for the Labour Party can be found in the papers which he presented to the British Library of Political and Economic Science (BLPES) at the London School of Economics several years ago, in Hugh Dalton's papers (also in the BLPES) and in the archives of the Labour Party.

Furthermore, Lionel Robbins and James Meade both kept diaries during their service in the Economic Section. Robbins' official diaries were written while he was in the United States attending wartime international conferences and immediate postwar negotiations, mainly for the benefit of his colleagues back home in the Section. They cover the United Nations Food Conference at Hot Springs, Virginia, in May and June 1943, the United Nations Monetary Conference at Bretton Woods, New Hampshire, in July 1944, and part of the protracted Anglo-American loan negotiations of September-December 1945. Written up daily, they also record preliminary discussions between British and American officials in Washington preceding the two international conferences and Robbins' personal reactions to wartime America. Meade kept a similar, but more personal, diary when he visited Ottawa and Washington as a member of a British mission to discuss postwar economic policy (including his own "Commercial Union" proposal) in September and October 1943. Meade also kept a longer and more detailed diary, written at weekly or fortnightly intervals, of his and his colleagues' activities in the Section from November 1944, when he was appointed to succeed Robbins at the end of hostilities, until September 1946, the month before the London Conference on Trade and Employment took up all his time. Robbins' three diaries were typed for circulation to his colleagues but not retained by them (except for a copy of part of the 1944 diary in the Keynes papers). They are now in his family's hands, and amount to the equivalent of some 200 pages of double-spaced typescript. Meade's two diaries are in manuscript, comprising the equivalent of approximately 80 and 500 typed pages, and are with his other papers in the BLPES, where his Cabinet Office diary at least has already been found invaluable by several scholars working on the 1940s. All five diaries provide fascinating insights into economic policy-making, in Whitehall and between American, Canadian and British government officials.

Second, *what sort of editing do these papers require?* The nature of the editing is in the first instance that of historical documents for the use of historians and other students of the period – the 1930s, the Second World War and the immediate postwar years in this case – that is, "making available in accurate and comprehensive reprints the raw materials of history...[L]etters..., memoranda, reports, miscellaneous documents...are assembled, dated, different versions are assessed, and finally what is judged to be the definitive form of each document is methodically transcribed and provided with an appropriate commentary" (Bowers 1981, 46). Such documentary editing has also been described as that of a "scribe, reporter, cultural archeologist [who] does not interpret [the documentary evidence] in the edition" (Badaracco 1981, 42). The editorial apparatus required is twofold: (1) explanation and identification of events and persons mentioned in the texts, and (2), by way of introduction, explanation of the reasons for the existence of the documents, the context in which they were written. But little of my editing experience with the papers of the Economic Advisory Council and of James Meade has been quite like that, so let me tell you what in fact happened.

I was first asked by Donald Winch of the University of Sussex to collaborate with him on an edition of some of the papers of the EAC – such as the Report of the Committee of Economists in 1930 – which would be of interest to economists and historians of economic thought. The editorial apparatus would be as I have described, with the introduction discussing the origins of the Council and the reasons for its failure to influence economic policy. The process of selecting the reports and memoranda to be published was to involve some research in the Public Record Office to ascertain the terms of reference and composition of the committees and the fate of the many reports (fifty-six in all) that they produced. As expected, the Council's proceedings were found to have attracted little attention in Whitehall and the Committee of Economists' report proved to be more important for what the economists thought than for any influence on the thoughts of officials or Ministers of the Crown. Contrary to expectation, however, the Committee on Economic Information and three related committees – namely the Prime Minister's Advisory Committee on Financial Questions in 1931–2, the Committee on International Economic Policy in 1932–3 and the Sub-committee on the Trend of Unemployment in 1935 – were the focus of considerable comment and significant criticism within Whitehall; even more surprising Treasury policy on several more technical issues in macroeconomic policy bore a striking resemblance to those proposed by the EAC economists. (I have not time or space to give examples; suffice it to say that I am thinking here of British exchange rate policy in and after 1932, British government proposals on international lending put forward at the World Monetary and Economic Conference in 1933, and Treasury attitudes toward the use of interest rates on the one hand and public works on the other in the event of a slump anticipated in 1936–7.) As a result of these discoveries the introduction of the edition of EAC papers grew into a book length manuscript to which were appended a few (ten only) papers – the reports of the Committee of Economists and three other *ad hoc* committees and six reports of the Committee on Economic Information – followed by a full list of EAC committees and a *dramatis personae*, part of which appears as an appendix to this paper. (The volume, *The Economic Advisory Council 1930–1939: A Study of Economic Advice during Depression and Recovery*, was published by Cambridge University Press in 1977.)[5]

Turning to James Meade, I was asked in the summer of 1985, at the end of a sabbatical leave in Oxford, to edit his collected papers for publication by George Allen & Unwin. I was handed four large box files – Meade's own collection of his offprints, pamphlets, reviews, letters to *The Times*, etc., which Allen & Unwin's economics editor estimated could produce two published volumes. At this stage Donald Moggridge and I had already undertaken to edit his Cabinet Office Diary for publication; also I had spent my year's leave in research on the monetary policy of the first majority Labour government in Britain, the Attlee governments of 1945–51. I therefore sought to include unpublished papers, written for the Labour Party in the 1930s or in the Economic Section in the 1940s, to which Allen & Unwin readily agreed. There will now be three or possibly four volumes of papers (academic articles, pamphlets, and memoranda – but not correspondence), with the Cabinet Office diary as the fourth (or fifth) volume. At least the first volume is intended to appear in

---

5/ The ten documents reproduced were thus explicitly selected on the basis of our interpretation of EAC economists' influence on British economic policy in the 1930s, and for each report the version reproduced was that most widely circulated in Whitehall at the time.

1987, the year of James Meade's 80th birthday.

What problems have I set myself in producing such an edition (apart, that is, from an early deadline)? There are at least two major ones – both relating to organisation as well as to selection of the documents reproduced. Meade wrote on a wide range of problems in most fields of economics: Keynesian unemployment theory, national income accounting, exchange-rate theory, open economy macroeconomics (which he more or less invented), international trade, price theory and welfare economics, growth theory, economic development, problems of income distribution, some aspects of industrial organisation, and, last but not least, the control of inflation. He has also always been as concerned with economic policy as with economic theory. As he admitted in his inaugural lecture at the London School of Economics in February 1948:

> My main concern in economics has always been, not with descriptive or institutional studies, but with theoretical analysis and, in particular, with the contribution which economic analysis has to make to the solutions of problems of practical economic policy. (Meade 1948, 1)

To this concern his 1936 textbook, *An Introduction to Economic Analysis and Policy* (second edition 1937), bears eloquent witness containing as it does lengthy and well-developed arguments for a large number of radical proposals for the solution of the problems of unemployment and inequality without any detriment to the quality or comprehensiveness of the treatment of the *whole* corpus of economic theory as it existed in the mid-1930s. This book has in fact provided the solution to both of the editorial problems I mentioned a moment ago. I have organised the papers, published and unpublished, theoretical and applied, into the five categories into which Meade's *Economic Analysis and Policy* is divided. He labelled these Unemployment; Competition and Monopoly; The Distribution of Income; The Supply of the Primary Factors of Production; and International Problems. I shall, reflecting modern usage, call them Employment and Inflation; Price Theory and Policy; Distribution; Growth and Development; and International Economics. In this way theory and policy papers can be placed side by side – for example, a memorandum written on the control of inflation for the Budget Committee of the Treasury in 1946 can be juxtaposed with his inaugural lecture as Professor of Political Economy in Cambridge on the same subject twelve years later.[6] Problems remain, of course: some papers cover two or more of the five areas, and open economy macroeconomics has to be placed in International Economics (though this turns out not to be too serious a problem since most of Meade's work on international problems was undertaken between 1947 and the late 1960s). A good example is Meade's first publication, *Public Works in their International Aspect*, published as a New Fabian Research Bureau pamphlet in 1933, which could be placed in the first or the last of the five categories. My solution has been to include it in the first since Meade's major concern in the 1930s was the unemployment problem. This has the satisfying consequence that his first published paper becomes the first in the edition. (A more extreme example of the multiple category problem is a long unpublished "Outline of economic policy for a Labour government" which Meade wrote in 1935 in the hope, which was disappointed, that it would be published as another New Fabian Research Bureau pamphlet. This dealt at length with monetary and fiscal policy, exchange-rate policy, and the nationalisation of industry. Again I have decided to place it in Part I on the ground

6/ "The Control of Inflation", June 1946, PRO T171/389 and Meade Papers 3/10, BLPES; Meade 1958.

that its overriding concern is with unemployment.)[7]

Other editorial problems I have encountered with Meade's papers are: (1) *selection*, (2) *copytext* and (3) *editorial apparatus*. With respect to selection I have followed two very simple criteria for published papers: major articles in major academic journals on the one hand, and on the other essays, lectures or pamphlets which present his policy proposals and his analyses of their effects. Most of Meade's academic articles were published in journals still regarded today as among the best in the discipline, particularly the *Economic Journal*, the *Review of Economic Studies*, and less often *Oxford Economic Papers*. Articles in lesser publications have been included where they illustrate Meade's views on policy issues. The task of choosing from the unpublished papers has been made much less daunting by starting from his own papers which include at least the first drafts of his Labour Party papers and copies of 45 papers which he chose to take with him when he left the Economic Section in 1947 (plus one he was forbidden to take),[8] and supplementing this with research in Labour Party sources and the Public Record Office (PRO). A high proportion of the memoranda survive in more than one version – hence the problem of copytext – but my researches (of the same kind undertaken for the EAC volume) have shown that in almost all cases the version in Meade's papers is the final version from his own hand and/or the version that was most widely circulated or influential so that Meade's copy will usually be used as copytext.

I intend to indicate the reasons for the choice of individual memoranda briefly in the edition, but otherwise the problem

7/ "Outline of economic policy for a Labour government", Meade Papers 2/9, BLPES.
8/ Meade Papers 2/7, 2/9, 3/2 and 3/10; B(46)11, Meade to Bridges, 24 January 1946, PRO T171/388; Norman Brook to Meade, 29 August 1947, Meade Papers 3/10.

of editorial apparatus only looms large in the publication of the Cabinet Office diary. Hundreds (or thousands) of references to officials, committees, ministers, memoranda, events and decisions have had to be traced, mainly in the PRO – I am extremely glad that the editing of the diary has been a collaborative project and that we have had the help of an able research assistant, Catherine Schenk. The diary will, therefore, be decorated with many footnotes, but in order not to irritate knowledgeable readers there will be a *dramatis personae* and a list of official committees on the lines of the *Economic Advisory Council* volume. Although these two appendices will reduce the number of footnotes there remains the question of the amount of information to provide in the footnotes. Should (or can) every single report, memorandum, minute or brief, however mundane, be identified? We have not yet come up with a satisfactory solution, but I suspect the eventual solution will be a pragmatic one – to stop at the point at which "diminishing returns" set in in the search for PRO references.

It will seem obvious that copytext is not a problem with Meade's Cabinet Office Diary which exists as a single manuscript. However, when placing the diary in the BLPES, James Meade specified that scholars should only see a photocopy of the manuscript in order that he could omit certain passages which might offend persons he had mentioned. We therefore took advantage of having a live author, who allowed us to read the manuscript and to add back most of the omissions although sometimes in a shorter form. We thus expect to have an "ideal text" which "comes as close as the evidence [which in this case includes the author's expressed wishes] permits to what might have been…the final form of his work made by the author" (Bowers 1981, 51). Another way in which we sought to take advantage of a living author was in the matter of spelling. For instance, should we remove inconsistencies in spelling or reduce the amount of capitalisation? Our author, however, has left that to our judgment, which is to follow the style Meade used in his books, most of which were published by the same publisher, George Allen & Unwin.[9]

I have deliberately not yet mentioned the editing of Robbins' diaries or of Meade's diary of the mission to the U.S.A. in September-October 1943. On these work, again in collaboration with Donald Moggridge, has only recently begun, but we have made the major decisions – specifically, that the editorial principles and practice will follow those adopted for Meade's longer diary. It should also be mentioned that at the outset, when the idea of editing Robbins' diaries was first broached to me in a conversation with James Meade, James suggested that his American diary should be published alongside Robbins' diaries. This we intend to do, and we anticipate the publication of a single volume of the four diaries, probably by Blackwells.

* * *

I have, I trust, said enough about the papers of Robbins, Meade, and the Economic Advisory Council to indicate why they are worth editing and publishing. Since a major interest of the previously unpublished papers is the light they can shed on the role of economists as policy-makers, as well as on the evolution of the economists' more theoretical ideas, I should like to conclude this paper by outlining some of what I think the papers reveal about economists as policy-makers in Britain in the 1930s and 1940s. I shall mention only one aspect of their contribution to economic policy in those years, namely how the economists associated with the EAC and the Economic Section made themselves useful in Whitehall.

9/ I have adopted the same principle in the *Collected Papers* where I removed minor inconsistencies of spelling and obvious typographical errors (and also completed or corrected bibliographical references) but otherwise left the papers as originally typed or printed. In the *Economic Advisory Council*, on the other hand, the historical documents were reprinted without modification or regularisation.

The EAC did not fulfil the role intended for it by MacDonald and probably served no useful purpose in the two years of the second Labour government. But in the aftermath of the financial crisis which swept Britain from the gold standard the economists of the Committee on Economic Information found a role, when the Treasury turned to them for advice on post-gold standard exchange-rate and monetary policy (Howson and Winch 1977, 95–105). Once the excitement had died down, however, the economists had to work to make themselves useful. The Treasury would not automatically turn to them for advice on day-to-day policy. The Committee had to try to make its regular reports relevant to the concerns of the policy-makers, which were often not those of the economists. In this they generally succeeded – though not invariably: in Keynes's opinion their November 1937 report was verbose, out of date, and confused, "a really dreadful document" (Howson and Winch 1977, chapter 5). Donald Winch and I did not print that report.

What about the wartime Economic Section? Here several things came together from the beginning: as in 1931–2 with a new set of problems the Treasury was more inclined to involve the economists especially when those on the Committee on Economic Information had recently been focussing their attention on the matters (notably rearmament) that exercised Treasury officials. With Keynes in the Treasury from 1940 to support the efforts of the Section, we see such major innovations as the official national income and expenditure accounts and the 1941 Budget which used the national accounts and Keynesian ideas on controlling aggregate demand (Stone 1951, 83–101; Sayers 1956, chapter III). But the Section had to keep up the momentum. One way it did so was in the area of postwar reconstruction which I mentioned earlier (using Meade's description). The Section and particularly Meade began preparing plans and proposals for postwar unemployment policy in February 1941, and Meade wrote the first draft of what eventually became the 1944 White Paper on *Employment Policy* in April 1943. In the last months of the war Meade and his junior colleagues were working out the ways in which the White Paper policy could be implemented, a process which continued under the Attlee government though it was now called "economic planning" rather than Keynesian unemployment policy.[10] There was also a management aspect of all this activity. To put the problem in Meade's words –

> The [wartime] economic section was in reality a seminar of young academic economists chaired by their professor, Lionel Robbins. Their day-to-day duty was to prepare essays – what in Whitehall are called briefs – on the basic economic aspects of the wide range of problems which came up.... How easy it would have been for a small academic group to be totally ineffective.... (Meade 1984, 19).

When Meade was asked in 1972 how the economists in the Section had become so influential, he replied:

> We had three great strokes of luck. The first was our knowing Keynes in the Treasury. The second was... [our] extremely powerful minister [Sir John Anderson] who read our briefs, and therefore throughout Whitehall we became people it was worth squaring with.... The third stroke of luck was Lionel Robbins.... Instead of being the enfant terrible which some people

10/ EC(S)(41)17, "Economic reconstruction", 26 February 1941, PRO T230/13; EC(S)(43)5 (Second Revise), "Maintenance of full employment", April 1943, PRO T230/15 and Meade Papers 3/2; "Employment Policy and Economic Forecasting", 14 June 1945, PRO T273/319 and Meade Papers 3/10; EC(S)(45)28 (Second Revise), "Economic Planning", 10 October 1945, PRO T230/18 and Meade Papers 3/10; Meade Diary, *passim*.

had represented him to be before the war, he turned out to be the most fantastic, able, restrained diplomatist. He used to instruct us, 'You never, never say to anybody in Whitehall, "I'll report you to my powerful Minister". You take any snub and just go away. Our success will depend on making ourselves useful. If anybody asks you to help in any department with any problem, you immediately do it.' The result was that by the end of the war there wasn't a single interdepartmental committee on economic policy at which there wasn't a member of the Economic Section present. (Meade 1972, 10; see also Chester 1951, 10–11, 14–16).

When Meade was appointed to succeed Robbins as Director he had to concern himself with staffing the postwar Section, since established academics in wartime government service were returning to the universities, and to foster good working relations with the Treasury and the rest of the Whitehall machine. His Cabinet Office diary is a particularly rich source of information on this aspect of the Section's life in the immediate postwar years, and records both successes and setbacks. By the summer of 1946 considerable progress had been made and Meade could write in his diary (on 7 June 1946):

The great event, for which I have long been waiting, was that the Economic Section were asked to prepare for the Budget Committee a full dress paper on the control of inflation. I had an uncanny feeling of having stepped in Keynes' shoes.... If we can pull this off,...we shall be on the road to control the economic system not by [wartime physical] controls but a general financial policy for the control of the main lines of national expenditure.

Although the resulting memorandum (already mentioned

above) did not receive an immediately sympathetic reception from the Treasury,[11] subsequent budgets were to confirm that a peacetime role for economists in policy-making had been accepted and established – but of course that did not mean their advice would always be heeded.

11/ "Control of Inflation", and Note by Trend, July 1946, PRO T171/389.

Appendix: Dramatis Personae

Anderson, Sir John (later Lord Waverley) – Permanent Secretary, Home Office, 1922–32; Governor of Bengal, 1932–7; Lord President of the Council, 1940–3; Chancellor of the Exchequer, 1943–5.

Attlee, Clement (later Lord) – Chancellor of Duchy of Lancaster, 1930–1; Postmaster-General, 1931; Leader of Labour Party, 1935–45; Prime Minister, 1945–51; member, Committee on New Industrial Development, 1931–2.

Clark, Colin – Staff of Economic Advisory Council, 1930–1; University Lecturer in Statistics, University of Cambridge, 1931–7; Visiting Lecturer in Australian universities, 1937–8; Under-Secretary of State for Labour and Industry, Queensland, 1938–52; Director of Institute for Research in Agricultural Economics, Oxford, 1953–69.

Clay, Professor Henry (later Sir) – Jevons Professor of Political Economy, Manchester, 1922–7; Professor of Social Economics in the University of Manchester, 1927–30; Economic Adviser to Bank of England, 1930–44; Warden of Nuffield College, Oxford, 1944–54; member, Royal Commission on Unemployment Insurance, 1931.

Dalton, Hugh (later Lord) – Reader in Commerce/Economics, University of London, 1922–36; Parliamentary Under-Secretary, Foreign Office, 1929–31; Chancellor of the Exchequer, 1945–7; member, Committee on Chinese Situation, 1930.

Henderson, H.D. (later Sir Hubert) – Secretary, Cotton Control Board, 1917–19; Lecturer in Economics, University of Cambridge, 1919–23; Editor, *The Nation & Athenaeum*, 1923–30; Joint Secretary, Economic Advisory Council, 1930–4; member, Committee on Economic Information, 1931–9; Fellow, All Souls College, Oxford, 1934–51; member, Stamp Survey, 1939–40; Economic Adviser, Treasury, 1939–44; Drummond Professor of Political Economy, University of Oxford, 1945–51.

Jewkes, John – Professor of Social Economics, University of Manchester, 1936–46; Jevons Professor of Political Economy, 1946–8; Professor of Economic Organisation, University of Oxford, 1948–69; Director, Economic Section, War Cabinet Secretariat, 1941.

Kahn, R.F. (later Lord Kahn) – Fellow of King's College, Cambridge, from 1931; temporary civil servant in various government departments, 1939–46; Professor of Economics, University of Cambridge, 1951–72;

Assistant Secretary, Committee of Economists, 1930.

Keynes, John Maynard (later Lord) – Fellow, King's College, Cambridge, 1909–46; Treasury, 1914–19 and 1940–6; member, Committee on Finance and Industry, 1929–31; member, Economic Advisory Council; Chairman, Committee on Economic Outlook, 1930, Committee of Economists; member, Committees on Channel Tunnel Policy, on Chinese Situation, on Economic Information, on Financial Questions, and on International Economic Policy.

MacDonald, James Ramsay – Prime Minister, 1924, 1929–35; Lord President of Council, 1935–7.

Meade, J.E. – Fellow and Lecturer in Economics, Hertford College, Oxford, 1930–7; Member, Economic Section, League of Nations, Geneva, 1938–40; Economic Assistant (1940–5) and Director (1946–7), Economic Section, Cabinet Offices; Professor of Commerce, London School of Economics, 1947–57; Professor of Political Economy, University of Cambridge, 1957–68.

Pigou, A.C. – Professor of Political Economy, University of Cambridge, 1908–44; member, Committee of Economists, 1930.

Robbins, L.C. (later Lord) – Professor of Economics, London School of Economics, 1929–61; Director, Economic Section, War Cabinet Offices, 1941–5; member, Committee of Economists, 1930; member, Committee on Limits of Economy Policy, 1932.

Robertson, D.H. (later Sir Dennis) – Fellow of Trinity College, Cambridge, 1914–38, 1944–63; Reader in Economics, University of Cambridge, 1930–8; Cassel Professor of Economics in the University of London, 1939–44; an adviser at Treasury, 1939–44; Professor of Political Economy, University of Cambridge, 1944–57; member, Committee on Trend of Unemployment, 1935; member, Committee on Economic Information, 1936–9.

Robinson, E.A.G. (later Sir Austin) – University Lecturer in Economics, Cambridge, 1929–49; War Cabinet Offices, 1939–42; Economic Adviser, Ministry of Production, 1942–5; Professor of Economics, University of Cambridge, 1950–65.

Stamp, Sir Josiah (later Lord) – Entered Civil Service 1896; Assistant Secretary, Board of Trade, 1916–19; Chairman, London, Midland and Scottish Railway, 1926–41; Director, Bank of England, 1928–41; British representative, Dawes Committee, Reparation Commission, 1924; member, Committee on National Debt and Taxation, 1924;

President, Royal Statistical Society 1930–2; member, Economic Advisory Council; member, Committee of Economists, 1930; Chairman, Committee on Economic Information, 1931–9; member, Advisory Committee on Financial Questions, 1931–2; member, Committee on Limits of Economic Policy, 1932; member, Committee on International Economic Policy, 1932–3.

Stone, J.R.N. – Offices of the War Cabinet and Central Statistical Office, 1940–5; Director, Department of Applied Economics, University of Cambridge, 1945–55; Leake Professor of Finance and Accounting, University of Cambridge, since 1955.

Source: Howson and Winch 1977, Appendix 2.

Works Cited

Badaracco, Claire 1984, "The Editor and the Question of Value: Proposal", *TEXT: Transactions of the Society for Textual Scholarship, 1 for 1981*, New York: AMS Press, 41–43.

Bowers, Fredson 1984, "The Editor and the Question of Value: Another View", *TEXT: Transactions of the Society for Textual Scholarship, 1 for 1981*, New York: AMS Press, 45–73.

Chester, D.N. 1951, "The Central Machinery for Economic Policy", in Chester (ed.) 1951, 5–33.

Chester, D.N. (ed.) 1951, *Lessons of the British War Economy*, Cambridge: Cambridge University Press.

Durbin, Elizabeth 1985, *New Jerusalems: The Labour Party and the Economics of Democratic Socialism*, London: Routledge Kegan Paul.

Gardner, R.N. 1980, *Sterling-Dollar Diplomacy*, New York: Columbia University Press.

Hopkins, Sir Richard 1951, "Introductory Note", in Chester (ed.) 1951, 1–4.

Howson, Susan 1986, "'Socialist Monetary Policy': Monetary Thought in the Labour Party in the 1940s", presented to History of Economics Society Meetings, New York, June 1986.

Howson, Susan and Donald Winch 1977, *The Economic Advisory Council 1930–1939: A Study in Economic Advice during Depression and Recovery*, Cambridge: Cambridge University Press.

Meade, J.E. 1933, *Public Works in their International Aspect*. NFRB Pamphlet No. 4. London: New Fabian Research Bureau.

— 1936: 1937, *An Introduction to Economic Analysis and Policy* 1st edition, Oxford: Clarendon Press; 2nd edition, London: Oxford University Press.

— 1948, "Financial Policy and the Balance of Payments". *Economica* 15, 1–15.

— 1951, *The Theory of International Economic Policy, Volume I: The Balance of Payments*, London: Oxford University Press for the Royal Institute of International Affairs.

— 1955, *The Theory of International Economic Policy, Volume II: Trade and Welfare*, London: Oxford University Press for the Royal Institute of International Affairs.

— 1958, *The Control of Inflation*, Cambridge: Cambridge University Press.

— 1972, "An Interview with James Meade". *Marginal Man*, 3, 3–7, 10–11.

— 1977, "James Meade", 8 December 1977 (in Meade 1987).

— 1984, "A Renaissance Man Remembered". *The Economist*, December 8, 19–20.

— 1987, *The Collected Papers of James Meade, Vol. I: Employment and Inflation* (ed. Susan Howson), London: Allen & Unwin.

Robbins, Lord 1971, *Autobiography of an Economist*, London: Macmillan.

Sayers, R.S. 1956, *Financial Policy 1939–45*, London: HMSO and Longmans, Green & Co.

Stone, Richard 1951, "The Use and Development of National Income and Expenditure Estimates", in Chester (ed.) 1951, 83–101.

Wilson, S.S. 1975, *The Cabinet Office to 1945*. Public Record Office Handbook No. 17. London: HMSO.

Index

Note: For discussions of particular editions see the entry for the relevant subjects – Economic Advisory Council, Jevons, Keynes, Marshall, Meade and Robbins.

MEMBERS OF THE TWENTY-SECOND CONFERENCE

Margaret Anderson, Faculty of Library and Information Science, University of Toronto, Toronto, M5S 1A1

A. Asimakopulos, Department of Economics, McGill University, Montreal H3A 2T5

Brad Bateman, Department of Economics, Simmons College, Boston, MA 02115

*G.E. Bentley, Jr., Department of English, University of Toronto, Toronto, M5S 1A1

R.D. Collison Black, Department of Economics, Queen's University, Belfast

Samuel Bostaph, Department of Economics, University of Dallas, Irving, TX 75061

Avi Cohen, Department of Economics, York University, Downsview, M3J 1P3

Adrian Darnell, Department of Economics, University of Durham, Durham, DH1 3HY

Frank Genovese, Babson College, Wellesley, MA 02157

*Michael Gervers, Division of Humanities, Scarborough College, University of Toronto, Scarborough, M1C 1A4

*John Grant, Department of Classics, University of Toronto, Toronto, M5S 1A1

H. Scott Gordon, Department of Economics, University of Indiana, Bloomington, IN 47405

John Hartwick, Department of Economics, University of Toronto, Toronto, M5S 1A1

Susan Howson, Department of Economics, University of Toronto, Toronto, M5S 1A1

H.J. Jackson, Division of Humanities, Scarborough College, University of Toronto, Scarborough, M1C 1A4

John Johnston, Department of Economics, University of Toronto, Toronto, M5S 1A1

David Laidler, Department of Economics, University of Western Ontario, London, N6A 3K7

*Richard Landon, Thomas Fischer Rare Book Library, University of Toronto, Toronto, M5S 1A1

William Long, AMS Press, New York

Randall McLeod, Department of English, Erindale College, University of Toronto, Mississauga, L5L 1C6

*Committee Members

*D.E. Moggridge, Department of Economics, University of Toronto, Toronto, M5S 1A1

Barry Norris, C.D. Howe Institute, Toronto.

Sandra Peart, Department of Economics, University of Toronto, Toronto, M5S 1A1

Mark Perlman, Department of Economics, University of Pittsburgh, Pittsburgh, PA 15217

David Phillips, Department of Economics, State University of New York at Buffalo, Amherst, NY 14260

Dane Rowlands, Department of Economics, University of Toronto, Toronto, M5S 1A1

T.K. Rymes, Department of Economics, Carleton University, Ottawa, K1S 5B6

Shouyong Shi, Department of Economics, University of Toronto, Toronto, M5S 1A1

Nancy South, Department of Economics, University of Toronto, Toronto, M5S 1A1

George Stigler, Center for the Study of the Economy and the State, University of Chicago, Chicago, IL 60637

Francis Taurand, Department of Economics, Université Laval, Quebec, G1K 7P4

*Germain Warkentin, Department of English, Victoria College, University of Toronto, Toronto, M5S 1K7

John K. Whitaker, Department of Economics, University of Virginia, Charlottesville, VA 22901

James Winter, Department of Economics, Acadia University, Wolfville, BOP 1XO

Chung Sik Yoo, Department of Economics, University of Toronto, Toronto, M5S 1A1

*Committee Members